100 Best Books
for Children

100 Best Books
for
Children

Anita Silvey

A Frances Tenenbaum Book

HOUGHTON MIFFLIN COMPANY

BOSTON · NEW YORK

For my grandparents, Ida Gravius McKitrick and
Albert McKitrick, who were passionate about books

For information about permission to reproduce selections
from this book, write to Permissions, Houghton Mifflin Company,
215 Park Avenue South, New York, New York 10003.

Visit our Web site: www.houghtonmifflinbooks.com.

Library of Congress Cataloging-in-Publication Data
Silvey, Anita
100 best books for children / Anita Silvey.
p.   cm.
Includes bibliographical references and index.
ISBN 0-618-27889-3
ISBN 0-618-61877-5 (pbk.)
1. Children's literature—Bibliography. 2. Best books. 3. Children
—Books and reading—United States. 4. Children's literature—
Stories, plots, etc. I. Title: One hundred best books for children.
II. Title. Z1037.S575 2004 011.62—dc22 2003056899

PRINTED IN THE UNITED STATES OF AMERICA

Book design by Robert Overholtzer

MP 10 9 8 7 6 5 4 3 2 1

Contents

Books for Beginning Readers ❧ Ages 5 to 7

Books for Young Readers ❧ Ages 7 to 9

Books for Middle Readers ❧ Ages 8 to 11

Books for Older Readers ✿ Ages II to I2

Acknowledgments

Three major university collections have preserved the history of children's books over the years. I relied on all of them for the examination of original material, and particularly want to thank Terri Goldich and Tom Wilstead, University of Connecticut, Storrs; Karen Nelson Hoyle and Jenny Hanson, Kerlan Collection, University of Minnesota, Minneapolis; and Dee Jones, DeGrummond Collection, University of Southern Mississippi, Hattiesburg.

Thanks to all of my students over the past two years, for their encouragement and enthusiasm, particularly to Simmons College students — Barbara MacLean, Katherine DyReyes, Bindy Fleischman, Stacy Howard, Barbara Leone, Paula Maloney, and Jean Todesca — for help with research details.

Around the year 2000, many people and organizations compiled their best-books-of-the-century lists. I am particularly indebted to Mary Burns for "Children's Classics" published by *The Horn Book Magazine* and to the panel that selected *School Library Journal*'s "One Hundred Books That Shaped the Century" — Karen Breen, Ellen Fader, Kathleen Odean, and Zena Sutherland. Both lists led me to many titles included in this volume.

Hundreds of people shared their own or their children's enthusiasm and insights. Particular thanks to Tracey Adams, Marion Dane Bauer, Marge Berube, Elizabeth Bluemle, Jessica Ferguson, Liz Fleming, Carol Goldenberg, Grace Greene, Betsy Groban, Judith Hillman, Thacher and Olivia Hurd, Colleen Kammer, Louise Kohoran, Joanne Lee, Stephanie Loer, Rick Margolis, Karen MacPherson, Hal Miller, Philip Nel, Natacha Pouecha, Karen Ritz, Maria Salvadore, Terri Schmitz, John Stewig, Jewel Stoddard, Duncan Todd, Pat Wroclawski, Hannah Zeiger, and to all those members of the publishing community whom I interviewed about specific titles.

Over the course of his career, Leonard Marcus has worked to

preserve the history of children's books. He answered many questions and led me to a variety of sources that I otherwise might not have found. I, and everyone who loves children's books, owe him a debt of gratitude.

Leda Schubert spent long hours discussing books and the shape of this list, and her patient and loving husband, Bob Rosenfeld, sat through many of these sessions. Although I couldn't incorporate his childhood favorite, *Terry and Bunky Play Football*, I am grateful for both Leda's and Bob's contributions.

Peter Sieruta served as the primary researcher for this book. His clearheaded analysis of books and his skills in finding material, no matter how obscure, made it possible to finish this project in less than a decade. It was always a joy to work with him and to discuss the contents of each essay.

As I indicate throughout this book, I believe that printed works result from team efforts. Some of the members of my team deserve special mention: Doe Coover, agent, and Janet Silver, publisher, for their early enthusiasm for the project; Frances Tenenbaum, editor extraordinaire, for going the distance and for always gently reminding me about the needs of my readers; her immensely helpful assistant, Elizabeth Kluckhohn; Jayne Yaffe Kemp, for her careful attention to the details; Bob Overholtzer for his design; and Megan Wilson, for long and devoted hours of publicity support. In memory of my dear friend Bev Chaney, I would also like to thank those whom he called "the travelers," who went on the road to sell this book.

Introduction

After being read *Goodnight Moon,* a young girl places the book on the floor and tries to climb into it. A parent has gone through *Harry the Dirty Dog* twenty-five times in one day, and then the child says, "Now read it to me again." For years bored by books, a ten-year-old boy picks up *Harry Potter and the Sorcerer's Stone* and works his way, feverishly, through five volumes. And as an adult, perusing classic poetry, I myself come upon a verse that my mother read to me fifty years ago. Although she is now dead, I can hear the sound of her voice and feel her presence in the room.

When it comes to children and reading, millions of such stories exist. Nothing in a child's intellectual development offers more pleasure or more excitement than a good book. Nothing lasts longer in memory than childhood reading experiences. And nothing ensures the success of a child more in society than being read to from infancy through young adulthood. Reading books to and with children is the single most important thing a parent, grandparent, or significant adult can do.

Because children are young for such a short time, we need to give them their literary heritage during these brief years. Just as every literate adult knows certain books, every child should know specific children's books. If we fail to present these books to children, they reach adulthood without a basic literary heritage.

The canon of children's books remains the best gift we could ever give our children. These titles motivate children to read: they include the best stories, the most compelling characters, and the most imaginative language. And they have stood the test of time, having attracted a wide and diverse audience of both children and adults.

The task of finding ideal books often seems daunting. In *100 Best Books for Children* I have sought to make it easy. *100 Best Books* focuses on a select group, books that should be part of every child's literary background, books that have been effective with children for decades. A family can actually work through the entire list in a few years, matching the child's growth and reading interests. A parent, teacher, or any adult can take these hundred books and introduce them to children with confidence.

SELECTION PROCESS

For over fifty-five years I have read, and reread, about 125,000 children's books. I first encountered these books as a child and began a love affair that has lasted all of my life. For thirty-five years, I have worked in a variety of capacities in the children's book field. Half of that career I spent as a reviewer and editor of *The Horn Book Magazine,* sometimes called "the bible of children's books," which seeks to locate only the best books published. The other half I served as a publisher, sifting through manuscripts to determine what should be released for children. I have written, lectured, spoken on television and radio, and taught college classes about children's books. I can most simply describe myself as a children's book expert.

Because my list of favorites includes several thousand titles, I winnowed it down significantly for *100 Best Books for Children.* To do so, I spoke to hundreds of individuals to find out what books they remembered from their own childhood and what books had been meaningful to their children. I consulted every published list of the best children's books. Then, over a period of six months, I read and reread all of the books that had an enthusiastic following.

As I worked, I envisioned an imaginary scene. I was setting out on a dangerous ocean crossing. I knew that a large number of families, with children and small infants, were also traveling on the ship. I packed my bags with great attention because my trunk could hold only a hundred books. Which ones should they be? As my luck had it, we all got stranded on a desert island for twelve years. Had I packed this trunk to make sure that these infants got the books that would educate them, entertain them, and pass on their rightful literary heritage?

I used several important criteria to make the final selections for

100 Best Books. I chose books of the last hundred years, 1902 to 2002. I selected only one book per author, mentioning others in the essays that accompany each choice. I focused on books for children in preschool to age twelve. Naturally, I was hunting for books that all children's book experts would agree upon: books that have communicated to children over several generations, such as *Charlotte's Web* and *Goodnight Moon.* I then chose other, more recent titles, less well known, that I believed maintained the highest literary and artistic standards and that worked extremely well with children. I believe that many of these more current books will become classics.

I looked for those books that demonstrated the highest quality of writing and artistic excellence, that had stayed in print in the United States, and that had exhibited popularity over time with children, parents, teachers, librarians, and booksellers. I then tried to balance the list to make sure I had representation for different ages, interests, genres, reading skills, and ethnic backgrounds. In the end, of course, the choice of books was my own, because I had to be able to recommend wholeheartedly every book in this volume.

I truly believe that any child or any family who reads all hundred titles will enthusiastically hunt for more books. As I kept reminding myself, we fortunately aren't stranded on that desert island. I hope *100 Best Books for Children* helps encourage the reading of hundreds of other books.

CONTENT OF ESSAYS AND BOOK

In the essays, I discuss each book, summarizing its story or plot, and then I provide the "story behind the story." In my career I have been fortunate to have known, interviewed, and spent time with the vast majority of the people who have written and illustrated these books — including mid-twentieth-century authors such as P. L. Travers (*Mary Poppins*), Robert McCloskey (*Make Way for Ducklings*), and Hans and Margret Rey (*Curious George*). In working on this book, I also looked at original manuscripts and drawings and talked to people who had helped in the publication process, giving readers an inside look at why these books were created and what happened to them as they went through the editing process and out into the world. Often these stories give an adult a greater appreciation of a book and provide material to pass on to children. Because I have spent my career behind the scenes, so to speak, I wanted to bring readers there as well.

Many of these books have won numerous awards. I've indicated only the two most important—the Newbery Medal, given by the American Library Association for the "most distinguished contribution to American literature for children," and the Caldecott Medal, presented "to the artist of the most distinguished American picture book for children." The award committees, members of the Association for Library Services to Children, can also designate Honor Books, or those books they find worthy and that were considered for the award. I've indicated books designated with these awards and honors in the book citations at the beginning of each essay.

Unfortunately, because my selections span a century, they sometimes contain the stereotypes or insensitivities of another age. In some cases, I have indicated these problems in the essay, such as the pidgin English spoken in *The Cricket in Times Square*.

Obviously, many of the books have multiple editions. At times, my recommendations refer to a particular edition. I prefer, for example, Ernest Shepard's rendition of *The Wind in the Willows* and Tasha Tudor's version of *The Secret Garden*.

Because I hope that *100 Best Books for Children* will only whet the appetite of children for more great books, I have included an expanded reading list, "Beyond the 100 Best," that a child might enjoy.

I believe three stories exist for every book: the one the book tells, the one behind the book, and the story of what happens when a child or family reads the book. So I have included a Reading Journal for families and individuals to record those personal stories. Nothing can be more precious over time, and spark better memories, than a record of the books we have enjoyed or shared with our children. (I would also enjoy hearing comments about your favorite books at www.anitasilvey.com, and I will post particularly well written and impassioned additions to the list on the Web site.)

All of the hundred books in this volume are my old friends. In the essays, I am trying to convey my enthusiasm for these friends. In doing so, it is my hope that readers will grow to love these books as much as I do. I also hope that this guide inspires adults to take these magnificent books and pass them on to children. "Only the rarest kind of best in anything can be good enough for the young," said the English poet Walter de la Mare. This single volume discusses the crème de la crème of children's books — the books that can truly make a difference in the life of a child.

Board Books

Birth to Age 2

Goodnight Moon

Written by Margaret Wise Brown (1910–1952)
Illustrated by Clement Hurd (1908–1988)
Published in 1947 by Harper & Row
Birth to age 2   32 pages

Upon awakening early one morning in 1945, Margaret Wise Brown wrote down the entire text of *Goodnight Moon* in almost final form, and called it "Goodnight Room." That morning Brown, or "Brownie" as she was known, telephoned her editor, the legendary Ursula Nordstrom, to read her the text, which Nordstrom accepted immediately for publication. In those days, editorial taste rather than publishing committees determined the fate of geniuses.

Margaret Wise Brown, who would write more than a hundred books for children in her short career, claimed that she dreamt her stories, and *Goodnight Moon* appears to be a case in point. However, Brown's creative dreaming followed years of intense training. A student at Bank Street College's School of Education, Brown began to explore writing books that incorporated the revolutionary ideas of Lucy Sprague Mitchell, the visionary founder of Bank Street. Both Brown and Mitchell believed that books should expose young children to the "here and now" world of their own home surroundings. Children need to hear about and see all the things that they feel comfortable with in their own world. So in *Goodnight Moon,* the mother and child say good night to all the familiar objects around them. Everything present in the great green room is part of a child's real world and reflects Brown's "here and now" philosophy.

After the telephone call, Nordstrom began searching for an appropriate artist for the text, but Brown insisted she wanted no one other than Clement Hurd. *Goodnight Moon* demonstrates how great books are made, and almost unmade, by seconds and inches.

For his original sketches for the book, Hurd drew his protagonists as a human grandmother and a young boy. This version went through several proof stages, but eventually Margaret Wise Brown and Ursula Nordstrom insisted that the characters be bunnies. Hurd relented; as the illustrator of *The Runaway Bunny* (also by Brown), he could draw rabbits like an angel. In fact, those close to him often said he looked like a rabbit. Hence, the resulting book, rather than being tied to a human environment, achieved an otherworldly, timeless dimension.

Hurd also accepted Brown's and Nordstrom's criticism of the cow in his original picture. He altered it anatomically so that no one would object to the udders. And on Nordstrom's suggestion, he replaced a map with a bookcase because she wanted to promote the idea of children having books in their rooms. However, Hurd worked out many innovative concepts that remained in the final art. Half-page black-and-white illustrations display all the objects in the room; but Hurd used only one piece of color art for the main scene of the book. That art was simply darkened, by degrees, by the printer. As the story moves forward — "Goodnight bears / Goodnight chairs / . . . Goodnight mush / And goodnight to the old lady whispering 'hush'" — the child and parent keep going back to exactly the same room, but each time a little more light has been removed.

Goodnight Moon met immediately with the kind of criticism that all too frequently welcomes our great books. A Harper sales representative wrote, "Frankly I'm having a tough time with [*Goodnight Moon*]. . . . As soon as [most buyers] see the size of it for $2.00 they throw it at me. They like the color, story, and idea, but will not touch it at that price. . . . I don't think we'll even sniff the quota. At $1.00 it would really move." But the book was not reduced to $1.00, and it did not really move for another twenty years or so. *Goodnight Moon* remained a quiet book; not until the 1970s did it gain a significant audience.

Although some critics dismissed the book as overly sentimental when it appeared, future generations have grown to appreciate the crisp language, clear geometric forms, and bright, bold colors. Children as young as eight months can appreciate the appearance of familiar objects in the art — such as the moon, the fire, and the mouse. A timeless book, almost like a child's evening prayers, *Goodnight Moon* has lulled millions of children around the world to sleep.

Mr. Gumpy's Outing

....

By John Burningham (b. 1936)
Published in 1971 by Holt, Rinehart, and Winston
Birth to age 2   32 pages

After graduating from Central School of Arts and Crafts in London, John Burningham began searching for work as an artist. Because no one would hire him, he tried developing a children's book. Fortunately for both Burningham and for children, that first book, *Borka: The Adventures of a Goose with No Feathers*, won Britain's prestigious Kate Greenaway Medal, given to the best picture book of the year.

Seven years later, Burningham produced another book that won the Greenaway Medal. In *Mr. Gumpy's Outing*, the hero, who lives on a river, first appears wearing a hat and huge boots. Mr. Gumpy travels along in a boat, picking up animals and children who promise to make no trouble. But, of course, they cannot avoid breaking their promises, and the whole crew ends up in the river before going to a sumptuous high tea.

Wonderful to read aloud, the book can be, and often is, acted out by a group of children. The predictability of the story sequence — "'Will you take me with you?' said the dog. 'Yes,' said Mr. Gumpy. 'But don't tease the cat.' / 'May I come please, Mr. Gumpy?' said the pig. 'Very well, but don't muck about.'" — encourages children to join in; it also gives them confidence as they begin to read for themselves. Burningham deftly balances brown pen sketches, quite free and expressive, with brilliant full-color art. He deliberately gives the drawings an unfinished look — so the child can have maximum freedom to imagine events.

Although Burningham had an opportunity to extend Mr.

Gumpy's adventures further, which he did in *Mr. Gumpy's Motor Car,* he deliberately avoided creating a series. Fond of his characters, he is still more interested in a new project than in repeating something he knows.

John Burningham believes that really great children's books "contain as much for adults as for children." Certainly, parents and teachers have enjoyed this watery outing every bit as much as children. And at the end, when Mr. Gumpy says, "Come for a ride another day," the child and adult reader will probably do so — many, many times. *Mr. Gumpy's Outing* reminds us that readers of all ages can be charmed by simple things.

The Very Hungry Caterpillar

By Eric Carle (b. 1929)
Published in 1969 by World Publishing Company
Birth to age 2   24 pages

A young graphic designer, Eric Carle had been tinkering with the germ of an idea for a book called *A Week with Willi Worm.* He wanted to use a unique book design, with holes cut into the pages, to show the progress of a very hungry worm working his way through all kinds of foods until it grows fat. But his editor Ann Beneduce was less than enthusiastic about a green worm as a protagonist and believed that Carle should use a more sympathetic character. When she suggested a caterpillar, Carle answered simply, "Butterfly." With these new elements, Eric Carle completed *The Very Hungry Caterpillar,* a book that has become popular all over the world.

In the story a winsome caterpillar eats a variety of foods until he finally turns into a butterfly. While showing a simple story of transformation, the book presents very young children with such concepts as counting, days of the week, and the life cycle of a butterfly, in bold, graphic art.

Carle made his debut as a children's book illustrator in a school textbook story, written by Bill Martin, called *Brown Bear, Brown Bear, What Do You See?* Later reissued for bookstores, the title has enchanted millions of children with its simple rhythm, rhymes, and brilliant art. For *The Very Hungry Caterpillar,* Carle played with the form of the book and developed pages of different shapes and widths — an experiment influenced by the books he read as a child in Germany. Although no printer in the United States could be found to manufacture economically a book with so many die cuts, Beneduce located a printer in Japan who was able to produce the book. Since that time, *The Very Hungry Caterpillar* has sold a copy a minute somewhere in the world, more than 20 million altogether.

Over the years Carle has gone back to reillustrate many of his popular volumes, including *The Very Hungry Caterpillar,* aiming to get a wider variety of colors and a cleaner design. In his studio, he spatters colored tissue papers with paint to create special textures and effects. After cutting the papers into the desired shapes, he then pastes them in layers on cardboard. Sometimes he uses crayons or ink to make the final touches. Carle works and reworks each piece, aiming both for scientific accuracy and for visual excitement.

In November 2002, Eric Carle, his wife, Barbara, friends, and colleagues opened the Eric Carle Museum of Picture Book Art. Tucked in the hills of western Massachusetts, at Amherst, the museum has quickly become a travel destination for families and school groups who want to look at Carle's original collages as well as rotating exhibits of other artists' work. After presenting children with one popular book after another, Eric Carle gave all of the children of the United States and the world another unique gift — our first permanent American museum to house original picture-book art.

Freight Train

....

By Donald Crews (b. 1938)
Published in 1978 by Greenwillow Books
Caldecott Honor Book
Birth to age 2   24 pages

While serving in the military in Germany, Donald Crews, a graduate of Cooper Union School in New York, created a design portfolio that led to his first two books for children — *We Read: A to Z* and *Ten Black Dots*. For *Freight Train*, which he both wrote and illustrated, Crews turned to a childhood memory of his visits to his grandparents' farm in Florida; there he watched and counted the trains that traveled near the house.

In a spare text, just fifty-five words in length, the author labels the different freight cars — caboose, tank car, hopper, box car, cattle car — which emerge in bright colors and bold shapes. At first stationary, the train starts moving in the second half of the book through tunnels, across trestles, past cities, and picks up speed until it blurs.

Ava Weiss, the art director at Greenwillow, brought Crews and this book idea into Susan Hirschman, the publisher of the list. As Hirschman looked through the initial sketches and layout for the book, she felt an enormous degree of tension. It seemed so perfect, and yet without the right ending, the entire book would fail. When she got to the final words, "Going, going . . . , / gone," she knew that Crews had succeeded in creating something extremely difficult — a book that works perfectly for the youngest of readers.

To prepare the artwork, Crews created stencils and then added blocks of color, so that the book showed both the design and color to advantage. The year of publication, 1978, appears on one of the cars as does "N & A," for Crews's children, Nanette and Amy. But otherwise words, images, and type have been kept to an absolute minimum.

Color, color spectrum, movement, and light are all explored in *Freight Train*. Even more important, Donald Crews gives very young children a book, naturally fitting their interest in trains, that blends simplicity and sophistication.

The Carrot Seed

....

Written by Ruth Krauss (1901–1993)
Illustrated by Crockett Johnson (1906–1975)
Published in 1945 by Harper & Row
Birth to age 2   28 pages

W hen it was published, *The Carrot Seed* contained one of the shortest picture book texts, a mere 101 words. The book began as an imaginary conversation that Ruth Krauss conducted with her neighbor, a five-year-old boy. Originally a 10,000-word saga, Krauss whittled the text away again and again. Sometimes cutting proves harder than writing; in fact, Ruth Krauss claimed that *The Carrot Seed* took her an entire lifetime to craft.

In this brief saga, a young boy plants a seed. Although he has been told that it won't grow, he weeds and waters it with care. "And then, one day, / a carrot came up / just as the little boy had known it would."

Ruth Krauss often terrorized those who illustrated her books. Even her editor, Ursula Nordstrom, sent letters to her addressed "Dear Ruthless." She once told an illustrator working on one of her books how much she disliked his initial sketches. The artist agreed that they needed to be redone; much to his surprise, Krauss then took all the sketches and dumped them into a wastebasket. However, Krauss believed that Crockett Johnson's illustrations for *The Carrot Seed* were perfect and could never be improved. But then, Krauss and Johnson — the nom de plume for David Johnson Leisk, the creator of the Barnaby comic strips and *Harold and the Purple Crayon* — not only worked together, they were also married.

The book has engendered many different interpretations over the years. Some skeptics believe it encourages children not to trust their parents; some maintain it tells children to do what they feel, no matter what anyone else says; many claim that the book speaks about childhood faith. Often called "the little book with the big idea," *The Carrot Seed* appeals, whatever its meaning, to the youngest of readers — who, like the protagonist, trust in the power of action and positive thought.

Picture Books

Ages 2 to 8

Miss Nelson Is Missing!

....

Written by Harry Allard (b. 1928)
Illustrated by James Marshall (1942–1992)
Published in 1977 by Houghton Mifflin
Ages 5 to 8   32 pages

On a train to Chicago in July 1976, James Marshall began writing and designing the pages for *Miss Nelson Is Missing!* in one of his sketchbooks. Much like the famous children's book character Harriet the Spy, Marshall always kept such a notebook within reach. He had been given the idea for the book at three in the morning, when Harry Allard called him, woke him up, and said only "Miss Nelson is missing!" Then Allard hung up the phone. Having been roused, Marshall began to ponder who Miss Nelson actually was — and why she was missing.

A more-than-generous individual, Marshall gave Allard the title of author on their books. Actually, for their collaborations, Allard often provided the story ideas, but Marshall, a consummate wordsmith, crafted each line of the text with as much care as he drew each image. His sketchbook lists a series of Allard's ideas about Miss Nelson and then shows the one that Marshall decided to pursue.

As Marshall developed the book with his editor Walter Lorraine, he spun out the story of a teacher, Miss Nelson, and what happens to her class one day when the wicked substitute teacher Viola Swamp takes charge. In a story that humorously explores the relationship of teachers and their students, Marshall provides readers with one entertaining episode after another as well as the perfect ending — showing the true identity of Viola Swamp.

A sense of spontaneity proves to be one of the hardest things for any illustrator to maintain throughout a picture book, especially with so many eyes — from editors and art directors to the production staff — examining the art. But Marshall always managed to make his books look as if he drew them effortlessly, even though his own thinking about the characters and pacing of the story took him a great deal of work.

In his sketchbooks, he refined text, layout, and character images until he got them exactly right. So at first Viola Swamp — who was based on Marshall's least favorite teacher — had daisies on her dress, then tulips, before being attired in her striking black dress with striped tights. But she always had long fingernails — as did the teacher of Marshall's memory — and looked, Marshall felt, like "Maria Callas with a fake nose."

The cover of *Miss Nelson Is Missing!* proudly displays the map of Texas. Growing up in San Antonio, Marshall maintained throughout his career a broad Western storytelling style. But he created his books in Boston, New York, and in his last years Mansfield Hollow, Connecticut. It was a background that allowed him to fashion books for a broad group of children.

Although James Marshall's books and characters — including George and Martha, the Stupids, and the Cut-Ups — have been loved by legions of children, he never received any major awards in his lifetime. But his books have endured, while the glitzier and more pretentious titles have long ago faded away. A class act always, he dealt with enduring topics such as friendship and the foibles of human life. He was a keen observer of human emotion; his books contain heart, wit, and some of the greatest characters ever created for children.

Madeline

By Ludwig Bemelmans (1898–1962)
Published in 1939 by Simon & Schuster
Caldecott Honor Book
Ages 2 to 5   48 pages

Written in rhyming couplets, *Madeline* opens with the memorable lines, "In an old house in Paris / that was covered with vines / lived twelve little girls in two straight lines. / In two straight lines they broke their bread / and brushed their teeth / and went to bed." The bravest, youngest, and cheekiest of these girls, Madeline fears nothing: mice, ice, or tigers at the zoo. She even faces the removal of her appendix with great aplomb — and proudly displays her scar.

Often a great children's book comes about because of chance, or an accident. In the case of *Madeline,* the accident occurred on a bicycle. While cycling in 1938 on the Ile d'Yeu, off the coast of France, Ludwig Bemelmans collided with the only car on the island. Consequently, he spent part of the summer in the local hospital, where he was placed "in a small white carbolicky bed. In the next room was a little girl who had had her appendix out, and on the ceiling over my bed was a crack that, in the varying light of the morning, noon, and evening, looked like a rabbit. . . . I saw the nun bringing soup to the little girl. I remembered the stories my mother had told me of life in a convent school . . . and the little girl, the hospital, the room, the crank on the bed, the nurse . . . all fell into place."

While living in Gramercy Park in New York City, Bemelmans observed a class, taught by a French teacher, of small girls. She gave them a daily walk in their muffs and bonnets around the park in rows of two. All of this material combined in the artist's fertile mind to produce *Madeline.*

Known for her tireless pursuit of talented authors, the editor May Massee first met Ludwig Bemelmans at a dinner at his home and published his first book, *Hansi.* But Massee and several other publishers turned down *Madeline* because it seemed too sophisticated for children. However, she did publish Bemelmans's sequels, beginning with *Madeline's Rescue,* and purchased the rights to reissue the original book.

The beguiling art (drawn from a child's point of view), the plucky character of Madeline, the perfect order of the twelve little girls, and the predictable and memorable rhyme have charmed readers by the millions for over six decades. Accidents happen, but geniuses like Bemelmans turn them into masterpieces.

The Snowman

....

By Raymond Briggs (b. 1934)
Published in 1978 by Random House
Ages 2 to 5   32 pages

In a wordless picture book, Raymond Briggs utilizes the potential of the comic book format to tell the story of a little boy who rushes out into the snow to build a snowman. Then, at night, the boy invites the snowman into his house; after playing together, they set out on a magical flight. But at the end of the book, readers are left with a deep sense of melancholy and loss — by morning the snowman has melted away. Children take great delight in reading this sweet, funny, and touching story solely from pictures.

As a young boy, Briggs had always wanted to be a cartoonist. At the age of fifteen he enrolled at the Wimbledon School of Art in London with the intention of pursuing this dream. However, he received an education in the classical nineteenth-century academic tradition — drawing still-life and figure compositions. Eventually, after even more classical art training, he discovered that he did not want to become a painter. But it took him some time to return, in books like *The Snowman,* to his initial dream.

For the setting of the story, Briggs used his own house and garden in Sussex, at the foot of the South Downs, a few miles from Brighton. The snowman flies over the Downs to Brighton, then to the Royal Pavilion — not to the Kremlin, as some reviews maintained. Because he was concerned with keeping a spontaneous and childlike feeling in the drawings, Briggs used only pencil crayons to prepare the art.

The creator of many books for children, Raymond Briggs often fashioned books that proved to be controversial. However, in *The Snowman,* Briggs stayed within the pure realm of childhood fantasy. This totally satisfying and emotionally moving book has been effectively adapted for television and is often shown during the holiday season. Its very success for over a quarter of a century demonstrates the power art alone, without words, in telling stories for children.

Mike Mulligan and His Steam Shovel
....

By Virginia Lee Burton (1909–1968)
Published in 1939 by Houghton Mifflin
Ages 2 to 5   44 pages

When the former dancer and newspaper artist Virginia Lee Burton tried writing a book for children about the adventures of a dust bunny — *The Trials and the Trails of Jonnifer Lint* — it was turned down by thirteen publishers. One of the declining editors, Lovell Thompson of Houghton Mifflin, suggested she spend time discovering what books her sons enjoyed. Burton read them *Jonnifer Lint*, and her older son, Aris, promptly fell asleep. Because Burton's young boys were fascinated by trains, steam shovels, snowplows, and trucks, she focused on these subjects for her next few manuscripts, which did get published.

Mike Mulligan and His Steam Shovel explores how the old or old-fashioned must adapt or change. Newer, faster models keep replacing Mary Anne, a steam shovel. But with her champion, Mike Mulligan, at the controls, Mary Anne proves her intrinsic worth, and she and Mike secure a safe home in a cellar in Popperville. Most readers, well into their adult years, remember the lines: "When people used to stop and watch them, Mike Mulligan and Mary Anne used to dig a little faster and a little better. The more people stopped, the faster and better they dug."

Burton had trouble finding an appropriate ending for *Mike Mulligan and His Steam Shovel*. One day, reading her latest version of the story to a group of children, a young boy, Dickie Berkenbush, invented an ending that Burton admired, in which Mary Anne remained in the basement of the building after it was finished. Burton gave him credit in a footnote in the book. Now in his seventies,

Richard Berkenbush remains quite proud of the role he played in shaping a classic children's story.

Although Burton created several other fine books — *The Little House,* winner of the Caldecott Medal; *Katy and the Big Snow;* and *Life Story* — her greatest contribution to the American landscape remains the saga of Mary Anne and Mike Mulligan, now with more than 1.5 million copies in print. Published in 1939 when World War II began, it presented then — as it does now — an optimistic and life-affirming vision of the world, as the old order gave way to the new.

Millions of Cats

By Wanda Gág (1893–1946)
Published in 1928 by Coward McCann
Newbery Honor Book
Ages 2 to 5   32 pages

In a story grounded in folklore, *Millions of Cats* tells of a lonely old man and lonely old woman who simply want a kitten to love. So the man travels over hills and valleys and finds not one — but millions of cats. Finally, the couple end up with one small kitten, who grows nice and plump and becomes the perfect cat for them. As simple as this book seems, it revolutionized the American picture book.

Rather than relying on the traditional picture book format, a picture on one page and text on another, Wanda Gág developed the double-page spread in this small volume. She used both pages to move the story forward, pulling them together with art that sweeps across the entire spread; her favorite illustration fell in the center of the book — with the old man carrying cats against the rolling hills. Every page contains a different layout; she alternated her broad vistas with intimate scenes, drawing the reader in.

A fine printmaker and friend of Rockwell Kent, Wanda Gág had worked on a picture book, the basis for *Millions of Cats*, in 1922 and 1923 but had found no publisher for her efforts. In March 1928 the editor Ernestine Evans saw a show of Gág's work at the Weyhe Gallery in New York. Evans asked Gág if she would consider creating a book.

Gág returned to her 1923 manuscript and extensively rewrote it; in the process the refrain "Cats here, cats there, / Cats and kittens everywhere, / Hundreds of cats, / Thousands of cats, / Millions and billions and trillions of cats" became more pronounced with each revision. She always complained that she had to finish the book in too little time; in fact, she had only a couple of months because the book appeared on September 9, 1928. She remained dissatisfied with the text and even made notes for changes in a printed copy of the first edition.

However, Gág may have been the book's most severe critic. Reviewers praised this fresh, brilliant gem, and for over seventy-five years the book has captivated cat lovers, children, and adults — in fact it has continuously been in print since its publication, longer than any other American picture book.

Lilly's Purple Plastic Purse

By Kevin Henkes (b. 1960)
Published in 1996 by Greenwillow Books
Ages 5 to 8   32 pages

From age ten, Kevin Henkes knew he wanted to create children's books. So at nineteen, he decided to take his art portfolio to New York City. To prepare for this trip, Henkes studied all of the current picture books in the Cooperative Children's Book Center in Madison, Wisconsin. He made piles of his favorite books and rated each publisher. Then he set up appointments to show his portfolio, seeing his favorite publisher first.

At that appointment — with Susan Hirschman of Greenwillow

Books — Hirschman asked how Henkes had decided to come to Greenwillow. He described his personal picture-book study. "Where's your next appointment?" Hirschman asked. On being told, she offered him a contract. "You don't need to go there," she said, "but can I call your mother before you leave these offices?" That conversation proved the beginning of a long and wonderful creative partnership. For many years Henkes went to the Greenwillow offices to sit and write in a spare room and to volunteer for any needed office work.

The character of Lilly — a wildly enthusiastic child who loves life and school and who wants to please — made her first appearance in *Chester's Way*. She moved into Chester's neighborhood wearing a crown and jaunty red cowboy boots — "I am Lilly! I am the Queen! I like everything."

Henkes decided to give Lilly her own story. While walking through an airport, he saw a little girl with a purple plastic purse and knew he had the perfect accessory for his mouse girl. In *Lilly's Purple Plastic Purse,* Lilly takes center stage in a story about the trials and tribulations of school. Although Lilly loves school and her teacher, Mr. Slinger, she hates being kept in her place. Using a rhythmic text and childlike humor, Henkes also incorporates comic asides that will keep adults laughing.

One of those rare creators with multiple talents, Kevin Henkes has penned many children's novels as well as other unique picture books, including *Owen* and *Julius, the Baby of the World*. All of his books come from the heart, wit, and soul of an extraordinarily sensitive human being, who continues to pursue his childhood dream.

Swamp Angel

....

Written by Anne Isaacs (b. 1949)
Illustrated by Paul O. Zelinsky (b. 1953)
Published in 1994 by E. P. Dutton
Caldecott Honor Book
Ages 5 to 8   40 pages

While reading a dictionary of historical American words, Anne Isaacs came upon the phrase "swamp angel." Then one day her daughter arrived home, complaining about pioneer days at school. Although the boys got to chop wood, the girls had to make quilting squares. In her mind, Isaacs saw a tiny woman in a dirty buckskin dress, with hands on her hips, who said in a Tennessee accent, "Quiltin' is men's work!" Swamp Angel had arrived on the scene.

In an original American tall tale, one much like those about Paul Bunyan and Pecos Bill, Angelica Longrider, a.k.a. Swamp Angel, becomes the greatest woodswoman in Tennessee. Taller than her mother at birth, Swamp Angel builds her first log cabin at the age of two. After many great feats, Swamp Angel takes on Thundering Tarnation, a black bear "with a bottomless appetite for settlers' grub." Eventually, she sends Tarnation up to the sky, where he is transformed into a constellation.

The editor Donna Brooks received Isaacs's unsolicited manuscript in the mail and loved the playfulness of the language, the humor, and the funny images. Brooks had worked with the artist Paul Zelinsky and thought that this manuscript might be something he could do easily — a project with a sense of play.

But the book took on a life of its own. Zelinsky focused on the 1815 time period, which reminded him of crude American folk art. To get authentic illustrations, he acquired a thin, cherry-colored, woodgrained paper. He then prepared and primed it, so that it wouldn't curl and could take the paint. But much of this paper got ruined, and eventually he had to order something else through a woodworking magazine. Although it proved quite thick, Zelinsky, long behind in his delivery schedule, painted on it anyway. However, he failed to let the paint dry before varnishing it, and the entire batch had to be saved by an art conservator.

Those seeking strong feminine heroines will love Swamp Angel, a character who demonstrates that pioneer women did a lot more than quilting. *Swamp Angel* reminds us that picture books often result from three distinct talents: the author, the illustrator — and the editor who insightfully puts them together.

The Snowy Day

....

By Ezra Jack Keats (1916–1983)
Published in 1962 by Viking Press
Caldecott Medal
Ages 2 to 5   32 pages

To our modern eyes, *The Snowy Day* appears to be the gentle, perfect story of a young black boy's love of snow. In it Peter dons a red snowsuit and explores his neighborhood during a magical snowfall. He makes tracks in the snow and snow angels, and he slides down a mountain of snow.

For the artwork, Ezra Jack Keats turned to the medium of collage because of the freedom and vitality it provided. Keats worked in blocks of color with collage scraps to augment the design: he found a piece of Belgian canvas to represent bed linen and spattered India ink with a toothbrush to produce a backdrop for Peter's bed. Because the artwork is so spontaneous and ambiguous, the simple images engender stories of their own. Many readers interpret the white space below Peter's sleeping face as the snowball he created that magical day.

Today it is hard to believe that critics virulently attacked Ezra Jack Keats and that *The Snowy Day* was one of the most controversial children's books of the 1960s. As the first full-color picture book to feature a black protagonist, the book quickly won recognition and the Caldecott Medal. During the late 1960s and 1970s, Keats, however, was accused of everything from stereotyped characters to having no right, as a white man, to feature black children in his books. Basically humane and caring, Keats was deeply wounded by all of the personal and professional criticism leveled against him.

A member of a poor Polish Jewish family, Keats had known his share of hardship and discrimination. Naturally attracted to minority children for his subject matter, he wanted to show the faces of those who were playing in his Brooklyn neighborhood. In spite of the severe statements made about him, he went on to create several more books about Peter and his world.

Ultimately, the very success of *The Snowy Day* encouraged the publishing of many other multicultural books. In choosing to place a black face against the white snow, Ezra Jack Keats helped to change forever the contents of books for our children.

Leo the Late Bloomer

....

Written by Robert Kraus (1925–2001)
Illustrated by José Aruego (b. 1932)
Published in 1971 by Windmill Books
Ages 2 to 5   32 pages

At first, the protagonist Leo hardly seems a hero. He can't do anything right, including read, write, or draw. With a very patient mother tiger and a very fretful father, Leo makes little progress: "A watched bloomer doesn't bloom." But one day, as his parents hoped, Leo blooms, and not only does his face take on a beatific smile, he happily proclaims to the world, "I made it!"

The author Robert Kraus knew nothing personally about late blooming. He actually sold his first cartoon at the age of ten to a local newspaper in Milwaukee. By eighteen, he had been published in the *Saturday Evening Post* and *Esquire*. Eventually he worked for *The New Yorker,* providing about fifty cartoons a year. He also wrote and illustrated a series called the Bunny's Nutshell Library for Harper.

Kraus loved creating stories for children, and in 1965 he began his own publishing company, Windmill Books, which specialized in picture books. For his first publications, Kraus drew upon his wide circle of *New Yorker* artist friends: Charles Addams for *The Charles Addams Mother Goose,* Jacob Lawrence for *Harriet and the Promised Land,* and William Steig for *Sylvester and the Magic Pebble,* which won the Caldecott Medal. Finally, Kraus decided that it would be easier to write stories for these illustrators, rather than hunt for material for them. For the young Filipino-born José Aruego, he created the saga of *Leo the Late Bloomer*.

On Aruego's early books, he usually was listed solely as the artist. However, even for those books, his wife and fellow artist Ariane Dewey, helped create the final artwork. Aruego drew the energetic, vibrant lines; Dewey added the color washes. As great artistic partners, they would work on many fine books together, including the exuberant, funny, and expressive *Leo the Late Bloomer*.

Now for over thirty years, Leo has given pleasure — and hope — to late bloomers everywhere, young and old.

The Story of Ferdinand

Written by Munro Leaf (1905–1976)
Illustrated by Robert Lawson (1892–1957)
Published in 1936 by Viking Press
Ages 5 to 8   70 pages

In less than an hour, on a rainy fall afternoon in 1935, Munro Leaf penned a short story on a yellow legal pad to be illustrated by his friend Robert Lawson. As his protagonist, Leaf chose a bull, because "dogs, rabbits, mice and goats had all been done a thousand times." The editor May Massee immediately accepted the collaboration. *The Story of Ferdinand* features a Spanish bull who doesn't want to enter the bullfighting ring. Rather than joining the company of other rougher and more aggressive bulls, Ferdinand prefers to sit under a cork tree and smell the flowers.

Even though this message seems harmless enough today, the story of the daisy-eating bull became the first American picture book to be labeled subversive. Because it was published at the time of the Spanish civil war, some saw *The Story of Ferdinand* as supporting — some as criticizing — Generalissimo Francisco Franco, and it was banned in Spain. Adolf Hitler ordered the book burned as "degenerate democratic propaganda." In the United States, the book was accused of promoting fascism, anarchism, and communism. But along the way, *Ferdinand* gained some admirers as well — including Thomas Mann, H. G. Wells, Gandhi, and Franklin and Eleanor Roosevelt.

Controversy always sells books; although only 1,500 copies appeared in the first year, by the second year of publication 80,000 had been brought into print. In 1938, *The Story of Ferdinand* outsold *Gone With the Wind* as the number one bestseller in America.

What has kept the book in print for over six decades, however, is the subtle interplay between the artist and author. To illustrate Ferdinand sitting under the shade of the cork tree, for example, Robert Lawson drew masses of silly corks, right from a bottle, into the foliage. Leaf and Lawson entertain readers with an author-illustrator pas de deux infinitely more satisfying than either the text or art alone. But as both author and illustrator believed, *The Story of Ferdinand* remains a heartwarming and funny tale for children — about a bull who, in the end, "is very happy."

John Henry

Written by Julius Lester (b. 1939)
Illustrated by Jerry Pinkney (b. 1939)
Published in 1994 by Dial Books
Caldecott Honor Book
Ages 5 to 8   40 pages

The original legend of John Henry, who challenged a steam drill with his sledgehammer, has been celebrated in song for well over a century. Somewhere between 1870 and 1873, the Big Bend Tunnel of the Chesapeake and Ohio Railroad was built through the Allegheny Mountains in West Virginia. In the well-known ballad, the ex-slave John Henry battles against the steam drill — winning the contest but dying afterward.

The civil rights advocate and folksinger Julius Lester — who performed with such folk legends as Pete Seeger and Judy Collins — and the artist Jerry Pinkney began collaborating in the 1980s on a series of books, including *The Tales of Uncle Remus,* which combined their distinct writing and illustrating talents. Generally a picture book originates with the author, but for *John Henry* Pinkney began the process. He had considered John Henry one of his role models since childhood — someone who gave him comfort and support in a world where almost every other hero had white skin. Pinkney and his editor, Phyllis Fogelman, hoped that Lester would write the text. But Lester truly needed persuading. Certainly, as a musician, he knew the ballad, but only after talking to Pinkney did Lester begin to see John Henry as a figure much like Martin Luther King.

Lester believes that children need "heroes and heroines. A hero is one who is larger than life. Because he or she is superhuman, we are inspired to expand the boundaries of what we had thought possible." He incorporated this vision into the text, which adds many layers to the ballad of John Henry, and even brings him to the White House to be buried. A children's book illustrator for several decades, Pinkney created panoramic settings for the book, which garnered for him one of his many Caldecotts. The artwork so vividly portrays the protagonist that the reader feels as if he can actually touch John Henry.

Although *John Henry* tells about the death of a hero, ultimately it celebrates his life. As the text so eloquently states: "Dying ain't important. Everybody does that. What matters is how well you do your living."

Swimmy

By Leo Lionni (1910–1999)
Published in 1963 by Alfred A. Knopf
Caldecott Honor Book
Ages 5 to 8   32 pages

While on a train from Grand Central Station to Connecticut, Leo Lionni invented the story "Little Blue and Little Yellow" to entertain his two restless grandchildren. Unlike many other grandfathers, however, Lionni had years of experience in the graphic arts and design, working as art director for *Fortune* magazine. After that trip, he decided to develop a book from his spontaneous idea. When an old friend, the children's book editor Fabio Coen, came to have dinner with Lionni, Coen accepted this first manuscript for publication. After that, Lionni became fascinated with communicating, through graphic images, with children.

Although Lionni created many fine picture books, *Swimmy*, his fourth, remains the most satisfying — with a strong rhythm in the text, a simplicity of action, and a very logical development. In *Swimmy*, a group of small red fish — encouraged by Swimmy, the maverick black fish — form a cooperative so that they appear to be one large fish. Because they have come together, they can travel the ocean and chase the big fish away. Throughout most of the book, the image of Swimmy is the focal point of each page. Then, in a very satisfactory ending, Swimmy becomes the eye of the group — the seer, the visionary.

Leo Lionni's stories, told in the form of fables, always contain strong messages; *Swimmy* conveys how strength comes out of unity. Although adults have sometimes complained about the didactic quality of Lionni's writing, children enjoy working their way through the meaning of his tales. Consequently, *Swimmy* and the other Lionni books have long been favorite choices for the classroom.

Like his protagonist Swimmy, Leo Lionni proved to be a seer, a visionary, who encouraged the work of other artists — such as the young Eric Carle, author of *The Very Hungry Caterpillar*. Lionni believed that "in writing for children you must step away and look at the child from the perspective of an adult." Hence, during the course of his career, he grew from caring grandfather to creator of highly graphic and sophisticated books for children.

Chicka Chicka Boom Boom

....

Written by Bill Martin, Jr. (1916–2004), and John Archambault
Illustrated by Lois Ehlert (b. 1934)
Published in 1989 by Simon & Schuster
Ages 2 to 5   32 pages

Bill Martin worked for many years in educational publishing, creating textbooks to help children learn to read. But he had an uncanny knack for writing stories, paying attention to the "rhythms, melodies, and sounds of language." Teaming up with the poet and storyteller John Archambault, Martin authored many books, including this delightful chant, in which the letters of the alphabet take a rambunctious romp up a coconut tree.

The artist Lois Ehlert had been developing several books on her own, including *Planting the Rainbow, Color Zoo,* and *Feathers for Lunch,* when her agent sent her the manuscript for an alphabet book. She read the text, which she found rather strange, and she thought, What would I ever do with this? She was about to send the manuscript back, but upon rereading it she suddenly was struck by the rhythm and dancelike quality of the text.

At first she thought she might turn the story into a fiesta party and put the letters onstage. Instead she decided on polka dot borders, which frame the action. From the endpapers, showing the letters in upper- and lowercase, we can follow each of these twenty-six characters as they frolic and play throughout the pages of the book. Each letter stays the same color so that the youngest readers, even those unfamiliar with the alphabet, can easily follow them. The capital letters serve as adults in the drama; the lowercase letters, as children. Created in collage made of cut paper, the clean and clear colors virtually sing out on the white background — much as the text dances and sings: "'Whee!' said D / to E F G, / 'I'll beat you to the top / of the coconut tree.' / Chicka Chicka boom boom! / Will there be enough room?"

So successful has this alphabet book become that many children and parents remember learning to read with it. One day while

Ehlert was signing books at the Chicago Art Institute, a six-year-old girl said to her four-year-old sister, "Oh, *Chicka Chicka Boom Boom*. That was my favorite book when I was a little girl."

Snowflake Bentley

Written by Jacqueline Briggs Martin (b. 1945)
Illustrated by Mary Azarian (b. 1940)
Published in 1998 by Houghton Mifflin
Caldecott Medal
Ages 5 to 8   32 pages

Born in 1865 in Vermont, Wilson Bentley loved snow. As a young boy, he kept a record of the weather and experimented with raindrops. When he began studying snow crystals under a microscope, he discovered that each had its own shape and design. He then set out to find a way to photograph snow so that he could preserve the beauty of individual snow crystals.

Several publishing committees rejected the manuscript for *Snowflake Bentley* — for excellent reasons. The book focuses on the life of an adult, and Bentley definitely does not qualify as a household word. Fortunately, the manuscript eventually landed in the hands of Ann Rider, who had a vision for the book. She considered the manuscript special, a beautiful piece of writing that touched her emotionally. As the publisher, I said simply, "They'll know Bentley in Vermont; make the book good enough so that those in the other forty-nine states will want to learn about him."

Rider and Jacqueline Briggs Martin started to create a narrative that told the story of Bentley's life, interspersed with factual sidebars. An innovative format, designed by Bob Kosturko, then received the careful attention of Mary Azarian, whose woodcuts had captured the beauty of Vermont snow and the Vermont landscape for decades. The resulting book, celebrating Bentley's accomplishments and showing his struggles, proved to be not only a moving tribute but inspirational as well.

One day Rider decided to read the book to her daughter Molly, who liked the story and said that she also wanted to photograph snowflakes. Then Molly added, "But I don't want to do it for my *whole* life." However, the basic theme of the book, following one's dream in spite of adversity, has been perceived by thousands of children.

Although picture-book biographies had been published before, *Snowflake Bentley*'s very success helped launch an avalanche of such books — many about people even more obscure than Wilson Bentley. Like Bentley, the author, illustrator, and editor followed their own passion, and children have benefited from their conviction.

Make Way for Ducklings

....

By Robert McCloskey (1914–2003)
Published in 1941 by Viking Press
Caldecott Medal
Ages 5 to 8   64 pages

After spending hours in the Boston Public Garden drawing the surroundings and observing the daily happenings as an art student, Robert McCloskey heard about a family of ducks who had stopped traffic on Beacon Street. He seized the idea and began to write a text based on this true incident. In McCloskey's story, Mr. and Mrs. Mallard hunt for a place to live, a place without turtles or foxes. After hatching her young near the Charles River, Mrs. Mallard sets off with the ducklings for their final destination, the Boston Public Garden, and disrupts a city to get there. But with a little help from a friendly policeman, she and the ducklings come home at last, to a small island where their father is waiting.

Although the story line emerged with some clarity, McCloskey soon found he could neither think like a duck nor draw one. After studying mallards for two years at the American Museum of Natural History in New York, he purchased ducks, which he brought home to a Greenwich Village apartment and kept in the bathtub. Raising a terrible racket, the ducks woke up at the break of day; McCloskey followed them around with a Kleenex in one hand and a sketchpad in the other. When he couldn't get them to sit still long enough, he actually gave them wine to drink. Eventually, all his diligence paid off in the final drawings.

A shy boy from Ohio, Robert McCloskey met the aunt of a childhood friend, the editor May Massee, when he went to live in New York. Massee published his first children's book, *Lentil,* and also encouraged this new project, tentatively called *Boston Is Lovely in the Spring.* McCloskey's vision for the book proved to be a bit more grandiose than his editor's. He wanted the book to be printed in full color and had rendered some beautiful watercolors of the park and the Swan Boats. However, sixty-four pages of full-color printing seemed far too expensive, particularly for such an untried newcomer to the field of children's books.

So McCloskey had to settle for only the green of the cover. He chose brown ink, so much warmer than black ink and closer to a duck's color, as his final medium. With this limited palette, he worked even harder on his drawings. He paced the illustrations, gave them a variety of viewpoints, and threw in aerial views to get a sense of space and movement. He worked to capture the feel of Beacon Hill and "the detail of the wrought-iron fence that a child would put his hand on or run a stick along as he walked by." To make sure he got the best reproduction possible, McCloskey drew his final art on zinc sheets, which then went directly on the press.

In the process of transforming the book, the names of the ducks changed from "Mary, Martha, Phillys, Theodore, Beatrice, Alice, George, and John" to the more sonorous "Jack, Kack, Lack, Mack, Nack, Ouack, Pack, and Quack." And May Massee's assistant suggested the infinitely better title.

Well reviewed when it appeared and the winner of the Caldecott Medal, the book has still faced its share of criticism. Over the years, some readers have objected to Mr. Mallard being a deadbeat dad. However, mallard fathers do leave the care of their young to the mother and fly away; she probably prefers it that way. So in this detail of bird behavior, as in the detail of a duck's bill, Robert McCloskey simply stayed true to nature. Of course, the subtle re-uniting of the family in the final scene has enchanted children since the book first appeared during World War II, when many youngsters were separated from their fathers.

In 1987, for the 150th anniversary of the Boston Public Garden, the sculptor Nancy Schön installed a bronze replica of Mrs. Mallard and her famous charges not far from the wrought-iron gates made famous by the book. On any given day in the city of Boston, hundreds of children can be seen lovingly touching these statues. Now rubbed shiny with affection, this physical monument celebrates the enduring power of *Make Way for Ducklings*.

The Tale of Peter Rabbit

By Beatrix Potter (1866–1943)
Published in 1902 by Frederick Warne
Ages 5 to 8   56 pages

Although written in the Victorian period, *The Tale of Peter Rabbit* contains little sentiment. The reader, as well as the young rabbits, learns at the beginning: "Don't go into Mr. McGregor's garden: your Father had an accident there; he was put in a pie by Mrs. McGregor." And so when the adventurous Peter wanders into the garden, he can have little doubt about the stakes of his misadventure.

The Tale of Peter Rabbit actually began not as a book but as a story told to a child. In 1893, five-year-old Noel Moore, son of Beatrix Potter's former governess, lay in bed, recovering from an illness. To keep him entertained, Potter sent him a letter: "I don't know what to write to you, so I shall tell you a story about four little rabbits." She based her knowledge of rabbits on her beloved pet, Peter Piper, who slept in front of her fireplace. At least seven publishers rejected her small book before she decided to publish it herself in a limited edition of 250 copies in December 1901. After the success of this private printing, Frederick Warne agreed to reconsider the manuscript if Potter would reillustrate the entire book in color. With twenty-seven delicate watercolors, the book appeared in the fall of 1902. Within the first year, the book sold 50,000 copies, an amazing number in 1903.

Living in a repressive Victorian household, Beatrix Potter drew and created her imaginary animal stories as an emotional outlet. She became engaged to Frederick Warne, the son of her publisher, but he died before they married. Potter continued writing and illustrating, creating twenty-three small books. After she finally married her solicitor at the age of forty-seven, she focused on breeding sheep and life in the country. Her creative energies appear to have been sparked by unhappiness rather than the deep contentment that came in her later life.

For over a hundred years, *The Tale of Peter Rabbit* has extended the vocabularies and reading skills of young children. Never out of print or out of style, the book stands as the second best-selling hardcover children's book of all time in America (second only to *The Poky Little Puppy*) — with over 10 million copies in print.

Officer Buckle and Gloria

By Peggy Rathmann (b. 1953)
Published in 1995 by G. P. Putnam
Caldecott Medal
Ages 5 to 8   32 pages

A boring lecturer on safety, Officer Buckle makes his audiences snore until he is joined by his beautiful and affectionate police dog, Gloria. As the officer reads safety tips with his back turned to the dog, Gloria dramatically acts them out, to the amusement of the students. Officer Buckle remains ignorant of the reason behind his increased success as a speaker until a television crew films the act. At first disheartened because Gloria appears to be the star of the show, Buckle eventually realizes that they make a great team. For added entertainment, the front and back end-papers of the book contain multiple safety tips, appropriately demonstrated by Gloria.

Although some books, like *Goodnight Moon,* evolve easily, others — even those that appear to be simple — take many drafts and an arduous revision process. In the second instance, the author-artist still needs to make the book appear spontaneous. Such long-suffering books remind one of a swan swimming; the bird looks beautiful and serene on the surface while its legs paddle furiously under the water.

No better example of a swan swimming exists in picture books than Peggy Rathmann's *Officer Buckle and Gloria.* An inveterate reviser, a perfectionist who worked for four years on this picture book, Rathmann herself often went through up to ten drafts of each page before submitting them to her editor Arthur Levine. Together they continued to revise, making five to ten more drafts per page. At several points in the process, Rathmann considered changing the size, shape, race, and even the sex of Officer Buckle. But with all this revision and rethinking, Rathmann still kept a free-flowing, spontaneous feeling in the final book — giving readers a story with brilliant timing and pacing, filled with joy and real childlike humor.

Much like its creator, the book possesses both humor and heart. Its final line, "Always stick with your buddy!" resonates with both children and adults. For that time in their lives when children want to know the rules, no funnier introduction exists than *Officer Buckle and Gloria.*

Curious George

By H. A. Rey (1898–1977)
Published in 1941 by Houghton Mifflin
Ages 2 to 5   56 pages

No publishing story reads as dramatically as that of *Curious George*. His creators, the German Jews Hans and Margret Rey, lived in Paris when the Nazis invaded in 1940. They could not get out of the city until Hans managed to find some bicycle parts and cobble two bicycles together. Then they threw their winter coats and several children's book manuscripts on the bikes, and against all odds they escaped, peddling to Marseilles, where they found a boat to Lisbon and eventually reached America.

In the original French version, George had been called "Fifi," but fortunately the American editor managed a name change. George's essential trait, however, endless curiosity that always got him into trouble, remained. In a series of episodes, George wreaks havoc wherever he goes. But he never strays far from his companion, the man with the yellow hat, who always manages to save him in the end.

Although *Curious George* received positive reviews when it was first published, it did not prove to be an overnight success. In fact, in 1945 six more copies of the book got returned than got sold. In 1958 *Curious George* finally sold more than 10,000 copies in one year, and its popularity has only increased over time. Between the 1940s and the 1960s, George's escapades appeared in six more volumes. Margret Rey served as writer and Hans as illustrator on all the books, although she did not always get title-page recognition. They also created many individual stories as well, such as *Spotty*, *Pretzel*, and *Whiteblack the Penguin Sees the World*, which was located after the couple's deaths and published for the first time in 2000.

Margret Rey served as the model for George, both physically and as a personality; much like a child, she was always asking questions. By the time of her death, the books about Curious George had sold millions of copies worldwide, and George had become an American icon. Like his creators, he had survived harrowing circumstances. He too was a refugee, welcomed during wartime, who became part of the American landscape.

The True Story of the 3 Little Pigs

Written by Jon Scieszka (b. 1954)
Illustrated by Lane Smith (b. 1959)
Published in 1989 by Viking Press
Ages 5 to 8   32 pages

According to Alexander T. Wolf, no one understands the true story of "The Three Little Pigs." Al simply set off one day to borrow a cup of sugar. "It's not my fault wolves eat cute little animals like bunnies and sheep and pigs. . . . If cheeseburgers were cute, folks would probably think you were Big and Bad, too." Standing in front of the houses of straw and sticks, he sneezes, blows down the houses, and finds himself with unexpected ham dinners. While confronting the pig in the brick house, Al gets arrested, but, he believes, "The real story. I was framed." Told in the newspaper tabloid *Daily Wolf,* Jon Scieszka and Lane Smith's rendition of this tale has delighted readers since it appeared fifteen years ago.

If an author does not do his own illustrations, it is usually the editor who matches him with an illustrator. However, Scieszka and Smith found each other — and then found a publisher. Scieszka's wife, Jeri Hansen, an art director at *Sport* magazine, introduced him to the work of an illustrator she had recently seen. The first meeting of the two men took place in a zoo, an appropriate foreshadowing of their creative relationship.

While hunting for assignments, Lane Smith showed his portfolio to the editor Regina Hayes. She found his work amazing but had no texts at that point to offer him. He then produced some manuscripts, including Scieszka's "The Tale of A. Wolf." Considering this meeting "one of the luckiest days of my life," Hayes worked with the pair on the book, which presents a classic fairy tale from an alternate point of view.

With the book an immediate critical and commercial success, it took the publisher several months to get ahead of orders. To date,

The True Story of the 3 Little Pigs has sold well over a million copies. Scieszka and Smith have gone on to create several other humorous books — *The Stinky Cheese Man and Other Fairly Stupid Tales, Math Curse,* and *Baloney (Henry P.)* — all distinguished for both the writing and the art.

Not only do children find the humor wacky and wonderful, but adults enjoy reading these books as well. All agree that this talented duo blend text and art together as well as any contemporary author-illustrator combination.

Where the Wild Things Are

By Maurice Sendak (b. 1928)
Published in 1963 by Harper & Row
Caldecott Medal
Ages 2 to 5   40 pages

Maurice Sendak found his way into children's books by decorating F.A.O. Schwarz windows. With his brother Jack, Sendak had created some wooden toys and taken them to Schwarz to see if they could be sold. Although the toys proved too expensive to be reproduced, Sendak was offered a job creating elaborate window displays. Because of a call from the book buyer at Schwarz, the editor Ursula Nordstrom came to the store, saw Sendak's work, and offered him a children's book to illustrate.

After creating art for almost fifty books by other authors, Sendak took up a project of his own begun in November 1955, a saga called "Where the Wild Horses Are." But since he couldn't draw horses very well, he tried to think of another character he might use — eventually focusing on "Wild Things." That idea brought back childhood memories of his Brooklyn relatives — aunts, uncles, cousins — who would come visiting and eat his family's food. They pinched his cheeks and cooed over him, saying, "You're so cute, I could eat you up." Sendak brought these relatives and the movie *King Kong* together in his story cauldron. As Sendak drew and redrew the Wild Things — at first quite skinny and undernourished — they gained weight and density.

In *Where the Wild Things Are,* the hero rages against his mother for being sent to bed without any supper. Banished, an angry Max wills his bedroom to change into a forest. In that forest he finds the Wild Things. After taming them and enjoying a wild rumpus, Max grows homesick and discovers supper waiting for him — still hot. Through his fantasy, Max discharges his anger against his mother and returns sleepy, hungry, and at peace with himself.

The book closely adheres to Sendak's philosophy of childhood and children. "From their earliest years, children live on familiar terms with disrupting emotions. . . . They continually cope with frustration as best they can. And it is through fantasy that children achieve catharsis. It is the best means they have for taming Wild Things."

This spare text, with only 338 words, is wedded to brilliantly paced art. As the reader moves through the book, the pictures grow in size; in the center of the book, all the double-page spreads have been devoted to the Wild Things and their romp. And then, as the story draws to a conclusion, the pictures shrink in size again.

Famous for saying to Sendak that his art had been created by "the hand of God," Ursula Nordstrom focused almost exclusively on revising the text with him, letting him develop the art with his own — or a deity's — sensibilities. Sendak kept refining the art and didn't deliver it until September for fall publication. Harper created special copies for reviewers but sent the book out into the world without fanfare.

Where the Wild Things Are engendered immediate controversy. Skeptics concerned themselves with whether the book would upset small children. The psychologist Bruno Bettelheim, who had not read the book, commented negatively on it in *Ladies' Home Journal,* writing that the story would increase the desertion fears of children. But the book still won the Caldecott Medal, and it quickly became the most influential picture book of the 1960s and 1970s. Bringing the genre to new levels of psychological realism, *Where the Wild Things Are* touched not only the children who read it, but most of the artists who entered the realm of children's books after it appeared.

Where the Wild Things Are has captivated children for forty years. Each new generation finds the same satisfaction and delight in Sendak's vivid imagination. The writer's favorite fan letter reads: "How much does it cost to get to where the Wild Things are? If it is not expensive, my sister and I would like to spend the summer there." Many children have spent summers or years in that magical land, and the cost is merely the price of this masterpiece itself.

Caps for Sale

By Esphyr Slobodkina (1908–2002)
Published in 1940 by William R. Scott
Ages 2 to 5   44 pages

When Esphyr Slobodkina was confined to bed by a series of childhood illnesses, she amused herself by cutting out paper dolls and doilies. Born into a family of considerable artistic ability in Siberia, she immigrated to New York in 1928, a refugee of the Russian Revolution, and soon became involved with the group of painters and sculptors who called themselves the American Abstract Artists. She showed her work with artists such as Arshile Gorky, Stuart Davis, and Piet Mondrian.

Because she needed to supplement her income as a fine artist, Slobodkina sought out the writer Margaret Wise Brown, who then worked as an editor for William R. Scott. In selecting a technique for a children's book, Slobodkina decided to return to her paper-doll and doily experiments as a child and presented Brown with nineteen paper-collage storyboards. Dressed is a swirling Bohemian black cape and a beaded, crocheted skullcap, Slobodkina impressed Brown with her outfit as well as her illustrations. Brown offered her work, and eventually the duo created four books together, including *The Little Fireman*.

But when Slobodkina decided to produce a book herself, she turned to a humorous tale that had been told to her nephew years earlier. In *Caps for Sale: A Tale of a Peddler, Some Monkeys and Their Monkey Business,* the subtitle sets the stage for the story. A peddler, wearing all his merchandize stacked on his head, goes up and down streets crying, "Caps! Caps for sale. Fifty cents a cap." Having no success, he goes to take a nap — and lo and behold some monkeys steal his caps. Each time he asks for their return, the mischievous monkeys mimic him, crying, "Tsz, tsz, tsz." The artwork for the first edition used only three primary colors. But in 1947 Slobodkina revised the book, adding in ocher, red, and robin's-egg blue. Both the colors and style of the art had been inspired by the work of the primitive painter Henri Rousseau.

Few books are so well executed for story hour and group sharing. The interactive nature of the text encourages children to participate as monkeys, mimicking the peddler and singing out, "Tsz, tsz, tsz." Although Slobodkina would pursue fine art and sculpture in a long life as an artist, her most enduring creation remains this fabulous saga about some monkeys and their monkey business.

Doctor De Soto

By William Steig (1907–2003)
Published in 1982 by Farrar, Straus and Giroux
Newbery Honor Book
Ages 5 to 8   32 pages

The stock market crash of 1929 ultimately gave children's books one of its finest practitioners. William Steig's father lost everything that year, and so Steig had to provide for the family. Figuring his art would be his most marketable skill, he began drawing cartoons and sold one to *The New Yorker* in 1930. Over seventy years later, Steig remained the longest-running contributor to the magazine, with hundreds of covers and seventeen hundred drawings.

But his children's book career didn't begin until he was sixty, when his fellow *New Yorker* artist Robert Kraus asked him for a submission for Windmill Books. Many fine books later, Steig got the idea for this book by asking himself, What if you were a mouse dentist, and a fox came to you as a patient?

The deft, white-smocked Doctor De Soto appears as the model of a good dentist. To treat his large patients, cows and donkeys, he climbs up a ladder or gets hoisted into the patient's mouth on a pulley. Although he refuses to work on dangerous animals, particularly cats, when a fox with a rotten bicuspid gains admittance Doctor De Soto needs to use all of his own cunning — and a little help from modern science. Readers watch with glee as the gentle Doctor De Soto and his wife outfox the fox.

Although William Steig's picture books always look spontaneous and fresh, he often talked about what hard work they were. Idolizing Picasso, Steig used a loose pen line, with mischievous abstraction. He began each drawing with a face, an expression. The narrowed eyes, drooping mouth, or raised chin always tell us something about the character and how he feels. Steig put colors and inks directly on paper, with no preliminary sketches or drawing.

Steig's texts, with deft and sophisticated language, have always been the equal of his drawings. Like Dr. Seuss, Steig has created a menagerie of characters, and his other books have many fans: *Sylvester and the Magic Pebble, Amos and Boris, The Amazing Bone, Dominic,* and *Shrek!* A master of character, language, humor, and playfulness, William Steig began working on children's books in his sixties, but with each book and each year — until his last book, *When Everybody Wore a Hat* — he grew younger in spirit.

The Polar Express

....

By Chris Van Allsburg (b. 1949)
Published in 1985 by Houghton Mifflin
Caldecott Medal
Ages 2 to 5   32 pages

A t the Rhode Island School of Design, Chris Van Allsburg began his career as a sculptor, with surreal and intriguing
pieces entitled *Brancusi's Dog* and *Sinking of the Titanic*. But to di-
vert himself while working on sculpture, he started creating black-
and-white artwork, which he exhibited along with his sculptures in
a gallery in New York. Often this work, executed in graphite pencil
with some charcoal, contained interesting scenes that invited the
viewer to weave a story about them.

His wife, Lisa, with encouragement from the illustrator David
Macaulay, decided to take some of her husband's work to children's
book editors, to see if they had any interest. Van Allsburg, naturally
shy and self-effacing about his work, would probably not have tried
this approach. She went to New York to see several publishers, who
asked to think about what they had seen. She then went to Boston
to see Walter Lorraine, David Macaulay's editor. Lorraine looked at
a drawing, which showed a lump in the carpet and a man raising a
stick to hit it (an illustration now printed in Van Allsburg's *The
Mysteries of Harris Burdick*) and said, "If he can get this much storytelling content into one piece of art, I know he can create a children's book." Lisa Van Allsburg walked out with the promise of a
contract — and the rest, as they say, is history.

By the time Van Allsburg published his fourth book, *The Polar
Express*, he had already won the Caldecott Medal for *Jumanji*. *The
Polar Express* began with the image of a train standing still in front
of a boy's house in the middle of the night. Then Van Allsburg
started asking questions. "In what direction would the train be going? Why was it the middle of the night?" He decided to take the
boy due north on a journey. That led to the concept of a train, called
the Polar Express, traveling with children to the North Pole on

Christmas Eve. After this journey, Santa and his elves greet them and give them a silver bell that rings for all who believe in Christmas. Van Allsburg used pastel oils on brown paper — an art form that made the book production difficult but that lent an otherworldly and mysterious quality to the art.

Immediately both a critical and commercial success, *The Polar Express* made the first of many appearances on the *New York Times* bestseller list in 1985 and won a second Caldecott Medal for Van Allsburg. With close to 4 million copies in print, the book sells a quarter of a million copies annually. With books such as *The Polar Express* and *Jumanji,* Chris Van Allsburg became the most popular and critically acclaimed children's book artist of the 1980s.

Dedicated to his sister Karen, *The Polar Express* shows a wonderful brother-sister relationship, one that mirrored Van Allsburg's relationship with his own sister. As is true of so many classic children's books, *The Polar Express* moved from the personal world of the artist into the hearts and minds of its readers. Because the book can be viewed as a statement about the nature of faith, it is often read as a ritual in homes at Christmastime "for all who truly believe."

Alexander and the Terrible, Horrible, No Good, Very Bad Day

Written by Judith Viorst (b. 1931)
Illustrated by Ray Cruz (b. 1933)
Published in 1972 by Atheneum Publishers
Ages 5 to 8   32 pages

At the age of seven, Judith Viorst began writing a poetic ode to her dead mother and father. Since both still lived, they weren't particularly pleased. However, as an adult author she continued to use the people that she knew as subjects. A mother of three children (Anthony, Nicholas, and Alexander), Viorst not only took the names of her characters from her family, she also drew the emotional content and situations from her sons' lives. Finding them fierce and funny, she made her characters like them.

Now in his mid-thirties, Alexander gave his name and perpetual situation to one of the most enduring books of the 1970s. As a child, Alexander had a lot of bad days — he fell out of trees and off chairs, broke his wrist, and knocked out his front teeth. At the beginning of the story, Alexander tells us: "I went to sleep with gum in my mouth and now there's gum in my hair and when I got out of bed this morning I tripped on the skateboard . . . I could tell it was going to be a terrible, horrible, no good, very bad day. . . . I think I'll move to Australia." His prediction proves accurate, and Alexander gets harassed by his peers, ignored, and harshly judged. At the end of the day, he goes to sleep, learning from his mother that others have bad days, even in Australia.

Bibliotherapy rarely produces a classic, but this book describes perfectly a simple childhood and adult phenomenon — a day when things just don't go your way. Because the events occur in one day, the book suggests that this day — this bad news — can be contained. Because it uses a light touch, it also allows readers to laugh at themselves and their own problems, just as they laugh at Alexander.

In her writing life, Viorst has switched with ease from writing various forms — adult humorous verse, magazine articles, and a *Redbook* column. When *Alexander* got adapted into a theatrical version with music, the multitalented Viorst wrote lyrics. Now with over 3 million copies in print, *Alexander and the Terrible, Horrible, No Good, Very Bad Day* has helped many a child and adult get over a bad day — even in Australia.

Tuesday

By David Wiesner (b. 1956)
Published in 1991 by Clarion Books
Caldecott Medal
Ages 2 to 5   32 pages

The editor of *Tuesday,* Dorothy Briley always maintained that David Wiesner came into her life because of some old furniture. Dilys Evans, then working at *Cricket* magazine, had decided to become an agent for artists, something new in the children's book field. While talking to Evans one day, Briley noticed some extra, used chairs in her offices. "Here," she said, "take these. You need them more than I do." Touched by Briley's largesse of company chairs, Evans accepted the offer, promising to bring her benefactor the first exciting artist she found. So one day Evans brought in some of Wiesner's early drawings. Briley always believed that David Wiesner and her association with him proved far more priceless than office chairs.

Briley and Wiesner created several books together before they worked on *Tuesday.* In a picture book using merely twelve words, a flotilla of frogs, flying on lily pads, set off for a day of adventures. Moving the story forward with double-page spreads and sidebars, and using an ultramarine blue to link each spread visually, Wiesner chronicles the exploits of these eerie frogs over the course of one day. And, at the end of the book, the reader learns that the next Tuesday a group of pigs takes to the air.

For his books, David Wiesner always develops some kind of a visual motif or theme. Then in any successful book, at some moment he says, "Aha! I've got it." While flying in an airplane, Wiesner started to sketch, working on a flying frog idea that had long intrigued him. He envisioned these frogs on lily pads and started to draw sketches of them in that environment. As he asked himself, "Where would a flying frog go?" images began to emerge. In about an hour the story had fallen into place, with rough sketches, as well as a title. Wiesner liked *Tuesday* because its "ooze" sound seemed to evoke frogs.

Early in his days as an art student at the Rhode Island School of Design, David Wiesner became fascinated with a different kind of picture book from the ones then being published for children. After studying the work of Lynd Ward, he knew he wanted to try to craft books with a minimum of words, or no words — books that allowed the pictures to do the storytelling by themselves. The winner of two Caldecott Medals, for *The Three Pigs* and *Tuesday,* Wiesner has always followed his own muse and continued his search for book ideas that maximize the storytelling powers of illustration.

A Chair for My Mother

....

By Vera B. Williams (b. 1927)
Published in 1982 by Greenwillow Books
Caldecott Honor Book
Ages 5 to 8   32 pages

When Vera Williams was a child, her mother could afford to buy a chair only on the installment plan; Williams longed to give her mother some marvelous gift that would take away her sad, overworked look. "When I got the inspiration to make *A Chair for My Mother* I had the wonderful feeling that I now had the power, as a writer and an illustrator, to change the past into something I liked better and to make it as a kind of gift to my mother's memory."

In the story, a young girl named Rosa saves her money to buy a comfortable chair for her waitress mother. Their furniture burned in a fire, and although neighbors have helped them recreate a home, they still lack a sofa and chair. Along with her mother and grandmother, Rosa keeps filling a jar with small change, and they joyfully empty it to buy a chair covered with roses. Although the family lives in a low-rent neighborhood, with nothing elegant and fancy, a supportive and vital community exists around them. Williams placed complex, colorful borders around the pages to show the richly textured life of the characters, despite their slim material resources.

After Vera Williams had been in the Greenwillow offices to show the editor Susan Hirschman her original design and artwork for *A Chair for My Mother*, she traveled, by subway, to a peace demonstration. But in the tumult of the day, she left the book on the subway, and then got arrested for demonstrating. When she was able to return to her creative life, she had to redo the entire book.

Fortunately, Williams always feels great enthusiasm for her books — which include novels, poetry, and other unique picture books, such as *"More More More," Said the Baby* and *Stringbean's Trip to the Shining Sea*. Williams has even been known to take her books to bed with her. Because she loves her characters and her creations, she fills her books with an incandescent joy. Believing that pessimists should write only for adults, she created in *A Chair for My Mother* a book with a joyful ending that celebrates families, neighborhoods, and a special gift from a sensitive and loving child.

Seven Blind Mice

By Ed Young (b. 1931)
Published in 1992 by Philomel Books
Caldecott Honor Book
Ages 2 to 5   40 pages

In 1961 when Ed Young, who grew up in Shanghai, China, brought his art to show Ursula Nordstrom of Harper, he dressed casually, as usual, and carried a stack of drawings, executed on napkins and scrap paper, in a brown shopping bag. The guard pointed him to the rear freight elevator, thinking him a delivery man. Even the receptionist hesitated showing Young into the editor's office. However, Nordstrom carefully went over the drawings, gave him a manuscript, and asked him to take it home and think about illustrating the book.

Some thirty books later, Young wrote a rendition of the Indian tale of blind men and an elephant and featured mice as the protagonists. On succeeding days of the week, each mouse, shown in a different primary color, visits the elephant. A mouse touches the foot, trunk, or tusk and declares it to be a pillar, snake, or spear. Only the seventh mouse, the white mouse, examines the entire structure and determines its true form. Each page explores color and shape against a black background. Some of the pages can be viewed different ways: for example, when turned sideways the purple page contains a profile of Ed Young's father.

Patricia Lee Gauch, the editor; Nanette Stevenson, the art director; and Young worked together on the book, a trio who maintained a high degree of artistic tension throughout the process. Young knew he wanted to use a pure black background and reverse type in white. Although effective visually in the final book, this design proved extremely difficult to reproduce on the printing press. An exquisite paper cutter, Young worked in cut-paper collage; he also played with expressive mouse tails, weaving them in and out of the black space. Gauch suggested that the white mouse, the protagonist, become a female. Stevenson found subtle endpapers and a binding to match the feeling and mood of the text.

The elegance, beauty, and power of this particular book comes from the way all the elements combine: illustration, storytelling, design, and bookmaking. *Seven Blind Mice* demonstrates the moral of an ancient tale: "Knowing in part may make a fine tale, but wisdom comes from seeing the whole."

Harry the Dirty Dog

....

Written by Gene Zion (1913–1975)
Illustrated by Margaret Bloy Graham (b. 1920)
Published in 1956 by Harper & Row
Ages 2 to 5   32 pages

One of the doggiest of dogs to grace children's books, Harry opens his saga by scurrying down the steps of his family's house, attempting to avoid a bath by hiding his scrubbing brush. Initially a white dog with black spots, he becomes a black dog with white spots as he plays in coal chutes and in the railroad yard. Harry gets so dirty that his owners don't recognize him when he returns — until he finally succumbs to the dreaded bath. However, he has not totally repented; in the final page, Harry slips his scrubbing brush under a pillow. Using a simple idea and narrative structure, the book achieves a perfect balance between text and art. In the case of *Harry the Dirty Dog,* that balance resulted from the talents of a husband-and-wife team.

When Margaret Bloy Graham arrived in New York from Canada, she met Hans and Margret Rey, the creators of *Curious George.* Because Graham wanted to illustrate children's books, Hans showed her how to put together an art portfolio, and Margret encouraged Ursula Nordstrom of Harper to take a look at Graham's artwork. Consequently, one successful married pair proved instrumental in the career of another, as Graham's husband, Gene Zion, developed texts for her to illustrate.

One day when Graham came back from shopping, Zion handed her a complete story, one that would be virtually unchanged in *Harry the Dirty Dog.* As an artist, Graham knew instantly that it had both a fine visual idea and a fine story line. "This will keep us," she said simply. In a couple of days, she developed the pacing for the story and the initial character sketches of Harry.

Although Graham loved dogs, the couple didn't have any. However, her aunt lived with an Aberdeen terrier and a Sealyham terrier. Graham based the pictures of Harry — short legs, long body, big head — on a combination of these two dogs.

Recently, a grandfather told me about his grandson, who had just been given a copy of *Harry the Dirty Dog* for Christmas. In the first day, the boy had asked his mother to read the book twenty-five times. This episode speaks to the enduring, and endearing, quality of this book, one with a happy ending that has beguiled children for almost fifty years.

Books for
Beginning Readers

Ages 5 to 7

Frog and Toad Are Friends

By Arnold Lobel (1933–1987)
Published in 1970 by Harper & Row
Caldecott Honor Book
Ages 5 to 7   64 pages

One summer Arnold Lobel, his wife, Anita, and his two children traveled to Lake Bomoseen in Vermont for a country idyll. As a refugee from New York City, Lobel found himself constantly terrified by the dangers of the natural world. A band of marauding raccoons created unsettling noises. When a bat flew in the window, Lobel hid under the bed. However, for the children the summer proved to be a golden time. They took to exploring a large swamp near the house and brought home treasures: a large green, shiny frog and two dour and dyspeptic toads. Some years later these two animals became the stars of a series of highly successful I Can Read books.

By 1968, after several years of writing and illustrating, Lobel personally felt that he had been writing at children, rather than for them. Then as he thought back to the Vermont summer, which had now taken on a roseate glow, he wrote the line "Frog ran up the path to Toad's house." From that moment on, the story seemed to pour forth, honest fragments of Lobel's feelings about himself and his children.

In *Frog and Toad Are Friends,* Lobel presents five stories about two complementary personalities. Frog demonstrates adult, energetic, and optimistic characteristics, while Toad, more passive and pessimistic, needs guidance and reassurance. In the stories, Frog tries to awaken Toad from a long winter's nap to greet the spring. Embarrassed by his bathing suit, Toad only attracts more attention to himself when he attempts to keep others from looking. Frog and Toad share a world of creative idleness — where they read aloud, drink endless cups of tea, and go for long walks.

Arnold Lobel believed that "Frog and Toad belong to no one, but they belong to everyone, every sector: rich children, poor children, white children, black children. Everyone can relate to Frog and Toad because they don't exist in this world." Ultimately, Frog and Toad belong to everyone because the book celebrates true friendship — a relationship that crosses cultures, ages, and backgrounds.

Little Bear

....

Written by Else Holmelund Minarik (b. 1920)
Illustrated by Maurice Sendak (b. 1928)
Published in 1957 by Harper & Row
Ages 5 to 7   64 pages

Having been told by librarians that children often came in requesting books by saying "I can read," the editor Ursula Nordstrom wanted to create a series of books for children at that stage in their development. However, when Nordstrom suggested this idea to various authors, none showed any interest.

Then one day Else Holmelund Minarik appeared at the Harper offices without an appointment. Nordstrom's assistant, Susan Carr (later Hirschman), came out to see Minarik and to look over what she had brought. The Danish-born author, who had degrees in education and psychology, taught first grade in a rural school and had developed books for her students. Minarik thought that her manuscript "What Will Little Bear Wear?" would work perfectly for readers at the end of the first grade or the beginning of the second.

Carr immediately took the manuscript to Nordstrom, who called Minarik that day. The next day, Minarik came back with the other stories that became part of *Little Bear*. With the added talent of Nordstrom's favorite illustrator, Maurice Sendak, the book was published in the year that Rudolf Flesch's *Why Johnny Can't Read* became a national sensation.

With a wonderful blend of realism and fantasy, the four stories in *Little Bear* appeal emotionally to beginning readers. Although Little Bear sets off on his own adventures, he always returns to his mother's love. After becoming an astronaut, for instance, he finds himself back on Earth with his own mother: "You are my Mother Bear / And I am your Little Bear, / and we are on Earth, and you know it."

Minarik concerned herself with all the details of the book, the space between the lines, the length of the lines (no more than forty characters), and the line breaks. She went on to serve as a consultant for the entire I Can Read series. The books that resulted — chosen for their story lines but published in a format ideal for children — maintained the highest standards of bookmaking and illustration of the day.

Little Bear appeared in the same year as Dr. Seuss's *Cat in the Hat*. Together these two reading series — I Can Read and Beginner Books — changed the content of reading instruction in America.

Henry and Mudge

Written by Cynthia Rylant (b. 1954)
Illustrated by Suçie Stevenson (b. 1956)
Published in 1987 by Bradbury Press
Ages 5 to 7   40 pages

Living with her grandparents in Cool Ridge, West Virginia, Cynthia Rylant experienced poverty, pain, and the divorce of her parents when she was four. "They say that to be a writer you must first have an unhappy childhood. . . . I think maybe some children who have suffered a loss too great for words grow up into writers who are always trying to find those words, trying to find meaning for the way they have lived." Cynthia Rylant didn't read any children's books until her twenties, while working in the children's section of a library. And then she read, every night, all night long, with passion and enthusiasm.

At first Rylant wrote picture books, but in 1987 she started to create a series of books about a boy named Henry and his 180-pound English mastiff, Mudge. Essentially, this book tells the love story of a boy and his dog. Henry and Mudge do everything together, and Mudge adores sleeping on Henry's bed. One day, because he can't wait for Henry, Mudge goes away for a walk by himself, gets lost, and finally lies down to sleep. With Mudge gone, Henry cries for an hour but then goes in search of his dog — and the two are happily reunited.

All of Cynthia Rylant's writing contains strong autobiographical elements. In the case of these books, Rylant's son Nate inspired the character of Henry. During the 1980s Rylant's former husband owned large dogs, the basis for the character of Mudge. Because of her familiarity with English mastiffs, Rylant made sure the art sketches accurately portray dog behavior.

"I had no self-esteem growing up because we were low-income Appalachian. . . . Writing these books has given me a sense of self-worth that I didn't have my whole childhood. I am really proud of them. They . . . have made me feel that I am worthy of having a place on this earth." Without a doubt, the thirty-some books about Henry and Mudge have made the earth a good deal better — and have made reading much more pleasurable for children.

The Cat in the Hat

By Dr. Seuss (1904–1991)
Published in 1957 by Random House
Ages 5 to 7   61 pages

The publishing trials of Dr. Seuss (the pen name of Theodor Geisel) should give any aspiring writer cause for hope. His first book, *And to Think That I Saw It on Mulberry Street* — initially called *A Story That No One Can Beat* — was rejected by twenty-seven publishers. Fortunately for the world, as Dr. Seuss walked down Madison Avenue one day to return to his apartment and burn the manuscript, he ran into an old Dartmouth classmate who had just been made children's editor at a small publishing house, Vanguard Press, and he accepted the book for publication. All those publishers had criticized Dr. Seuss's book as "too different" because he used verse and words in an outrageous manner. But the author proved to be right in the end. Children loved his humor, the vitality of his characters, and the energy of his verse.

Dr. Seuss always claimed that he got his book ideas "in Switzerland near the Forka Pass. There is a little town called Gletch, and two thousand feet up above Gletch there is a smaller hamlet called Uber Gletch. . . . I wander around and talk to the people in the street. They are very strange people, and I get my ideas from them." But *The Cat in the Hat* came into being in an entirely different way, and Dr. Seuss always associated it with an elevator.

One spring day in 1955, Dr. Seuss rode in the brass cage of the ancient elevator at 2 Park Street in Boston, the home of Houghton Mifflin. He found himself a guest in the elevator, which shuddered and whined as it rose and descended, at the invitation of William Spaulding, who directed Houghton's educational division.

Spaulding wanted to improve the nation's literacy, and he believed that someone like Dr. Seuss, with his ability to communicate with children, should be wed to sound reading theory. What he proposed over dinner was that the author write a book that first-graders couldn't put down, a book that used just a few hundred words geared to the grade level.

Bennett Cerf of Random House, Dr. Seuss's publisher, agreed that the writer could create the book for Houghton's educational division, if Random House controlled rights for a bookstore edition. So Dr. Seuss set out to fashion a book, reading the list of words forty times and getting more and more discouraged. "It was like trying to make a strudel without any strudel," he said. "The only job I ever tackled that I found more difficult was when I wrote the Baedeker guide Eskimos use when they travel in Siam." He decided that the first two rhyming words that he located would make up the title — *cat* and *hat*.

It took a year to write the text, which depended on only 220 words. However, in the end it contained the usual Seussian exuberance: "'I know some new tricks' / Said the Cat in the Hat. / 'A lot of good tricks. / I will show them to you. / Your mother / Will not mind at all if I do.'" Dr. Seuss drew as he wrote, and an elongated feline with bowtie and stovepipe hat emerged, one of the best-loved members of the Seuss menagerie. The cat arrives one day to entertain two young children. As the rhyme spins out of control, so do the antics of the mayhem-making cat, and chaos ensues. But before Mother returns, the cat cleans up everything, leaving the children to ponder whether or not to tell her what happened.

When the book appeared in the Houghton Mifflin reading series, it barely made ripples. But when the bookstore edition got published, it received acclaim as an innovative masterpiece. The book jacket carried the statement that "many children . . . will discover for the first time that they don't need to be read to anymore." The "most influential first-grade reader since McGuffey," the book within three years sold a million copies. Today, with over 7 million copies in print, *The Cat in the Hat* holds a place among the top ten best-selling children's hardcover books of all time. Random House even hired Seuss to direct an enterprise called Beginner Books. Suddenly American children learning to read were being introduced to an entirely different kind of story — one that would make the Dick, Jane, and Spot chronicles a relic of the 1950s. Seuss went on to create other favorites in this series, including *Green Eggs and Ham*, which contains only fifty words.

In his children's book career, which would span over half a century, Dr. Seuss imagined the most amazing cast of characters — Horton, Bartholomew Cubbins, the Grinch — ever to emerge from one mind. He would pen brilliant picture books that have no equal in sheer, outrageous nonsense. And in his role as the pied piper of children's books, he would beguile young children, by legions, into reading.

Books for Young Readers

Ages 7 to 9

Ramona the Pest

Written by Beverly Cleary (b. 1917)
Illustrated by Louis Darling (1916–1970)
Published in 1968 by William Morrow
Ages 7 to 9   192 pages

Beverly Cleary's Ramona Quimby and Henry Huggins novels celebrate the ordinary trials and tribulations of childhood. Had she not written her memoirs in *A Girl from Yamhill*, the world might well believe she was endowed, as are her protagonists, with a truly happy childhood. As a child, she experienced the Depression, extreme poverty, and isolation in moving from a farm community to Portland, Oregon. But the chief villain of her childhood, one never reconstructed in Cleary's fiction, proved to be an unloving, judgmental mother. Hence Cleary's books represent the childhood she would like to have had, not the one that she actually knew.

Critics have described *Ramona the Pest* as a girl's experiences in meeting the Establishment. In this book, Ramona begins kindergarten and discovers all the joys of a new teacher, classmates with springy curls, challenging games like Gray Duck, and the endless possibilities of rest time. In Beverly Cleary's real life, she met the Establishment in the 1920s when she had to leave the family farm for the big city. A city school classroom came as quite a shock to her.

Cleary thought about *Ramona the Pest* for fifteen years before writing the book. In a New York taxi in 1953, her editor suggested that Cleary develop a story about Ramona, a minor character in the Henry Huggins books. She dismissed this idea and continued to work on other projects. But she found that Ramona, until then making only cameo appearances, began to take on a life of her own.

So in 1968, Beverly Cleary picked up a sheet of paper and began with a title, *Ramona the Pest*. "The story of Ramona's clash with the school system, her eagerness for attention, her stubbornness, her misunderstandings, her fears, her longing to love and be loved, almost seemed to write itself."

The children's book author Elizabeth Enright once wrote that true fiction comprises both wish and memory. In *Ramona the Pest*, Beverly Cleary combined her life experiences and her wish for a happy, satisfying childhood to create one of the most functional families in children's literature as well as one of the best-loved children's book characters, the irrepressible Ramona Quimby.

Sadako and the Thousand Paper Cranes

Written by Eleanor Coerr (b. 1922)
Illustrated by Ronald Himler (b. 1937)
Published in 1977 by G. P. Putnam
Ages 7 to 9   65 pages

Often called the "Anne Frank of Hiroshima," Sadako Sasaki, an athletic, lively, twelve-year-old girl, the star of her school's running team, contracted leukemia, the atomic bomb disease. Told to fold paper cranes — "If a sick person folds one thousand paper cranes, the gods will grant her wish and make her healthy again" — Sadako tried to create a thousand but died before she succeeded.

Eleanor Coerr, a journalist who also wrote children's stories, visited Japan for the first time in 1949. She spent three years there, interviewing citizens about their post–World War II experiences, living with a Japanese farm family, and developing an empathy for the victims of the war, particularly those affected in the brutal aftermath of the atomic bomb. Eventually marrying a career diplomat and ambassador, she returned to Japan in the 1960s and visited Hiroshima Peace Park, where a statue honoring Sadako (1943–1955) had been adorned with thousands of paper cranes. At the base stood an engraving: THIS IS OUR CRY, THIS IS OUR PRAYER; PEACE IN THE WORLD.

Inspired by this statue, she began to research Sadako's life and found a volume of her letters, *Kokeshi*, which had become widely known in Japan. Returning to the States, Coerr became a children's librarian and wrote more children's books. For her eighth book, she pulled together the material gathered in Japan to present a touching story, told in a straightforward manner, that speaks directly to young readers. Its very simplicity and its ability to show the tragedy of war as it affects one brave child make it a perennial classroom favorite. Teachers often include the folding of a thousand paper cranes as part of the reading exercises.

Published quietly, to excellent reviews, *Sadako and the Thousand Paper Cranes* has increased in popularity over the years and has sold about 1.5 million copies in paperback. On Peace Day, August 6, Japanese children place thousands of cranes at Sadako's statue. Because of this slim book, in print for over a quarter of a century, American children have grown to understand the significance of Sadako's death and her life — and the aftermath of war.

Morning Girl

By Michael Dorris (1945–1997)
Published in 1992 by Hyperion
Ages 7 to 9   74 pages

Of a mixed background — French, Irish, and Modoc — Michael Dorris spent time on various Indian reservations in the Pacific Northwest. After receiving a degree in anthropology from Yale, he founded the Native American Studies Program at Dartmouth College in 1972. Although Dorris basically pursued a career writing for adults — *The Broken Cord, A Yellow Raft in Blue Water,* and *The Crown of Columbus,* with his wife, Louise Erdrich — in the 1990s he penned three very brief novels for young readers.

While working on *The Crown of Columbus,* Dorris became intrigued by the Taino people, who first greeted Columbus in the New World. Nonliterate hunter-gatherers, the Taino faced extermination by the diseases that the Spaniards brought with them. Believing that history distorts reality and that important groups have not been represented in history, Dorris also knew that a great cause does not make a readable book for children. To write for them, he had to create characters that children would empathize with. When he was a child, Dorris seldom identified with the stereotypical Indians in the books he read — they were not the kind of children he wanted to play with or to know.

In *Morning Girl,* the story evolves in two voices — Morning Girl, twelve, and Star Boy, ten, brother and sister; one loves the day, the other the night. Their vision of life seems both simple and holistic; they live in a natural world that they delight in and understand. But they must survive the grief of their mother's miscarriage and a tropical storm that almost destroys Star Boy. They emerge as magnificent children — independent, strong, and curious. Then in a postscript at the end of the book, the reader learns a horrible truth: as Christopher Columbus writes, "They should be good and intelligent servants." We have grown to love and care for two Taino children whose entire civilization will soon come to an abrupt end.

A slim volume, *Morning Girl* changes the way readers look at the discovery of America. It causes them to care about a Native American boy and girl. Michael Dorris so skillfully evolves this narrative that readers look at history differently after they have finished this impassioned novel.

The Hundred Dresses

Written by Eleanor Estes (1906–1988)
Illustrated by Louis Slobodkin (1903–1975)
Published in 1944 by Harcourt Brace
Newbery Honor Book
Ages 7 to 9   81 pages

Writers rarely explore the issues of class and money in books for children. Much like religion and politics, these topics, although close to the hearts of many children, appear quite infrequently in their books.

Eleanor Estes waded into these murky waters with a slight, thirty-two-page manuscript, which took her a mere six months to complete. Eventually, extended by Louis Slobodkin's evocative watercolors, and refined in the editing process by Margaret McElderry, *The Hundred Dresses* became a small book, eighty-one pages in length but deep in meaning and significance.

In *The Hundred Dresses*, a group of fourth-grade girls taunt a poor classmate, Wanda Petronski, a Polish girl who wears the same faded blue dress each day. The leading bully, a rich girl named Peggy, eggs on her sidekick Maddie, who receives Peggy's hand-me-downs. In the face of her classmates' cruelty, Wanda claims to own a hundred dresses. And in the denouement, we find that she does — the ones that she has drawn herself.

Eleanor Estes focused on Maddie as the protagonist of the book. Maddie knows that abusing Wanda is morally wrong, but she is afraid to anger Peggy and act on her own. The book demonstrates the golden rule, that one should treat others the way one would want to be treated oneself. And, as the book shows, often children get no second chance to apologize for behavior. In the end, the reader experiences guilt and remorse, in bearable doses, by observing the feelings of believable children.

Louis Slobodkin's art brilliantly evokes the range of emotions in the text — from the bright autumns to the melancholy of wronged innocence. A sculptor turned illustrator, Slobodkin had worked with Estes on her popular books about the Moffats, and in 1944 Slobodkin accepted the Caldecott Medal for his rendition of James Thurber's *Many Moons*. Although these books remained popular for many years, ultimately Estes and Slobodkin's collaboration on *The Hundred Dresses* has best stood the test of time.

After all these years, *The Hundred Dresses* remains a three-handkerchief book. It always succeeds in response to the request "Can we read a sad book?"

My Father's Dragon

....

Written by Ruth Stiles Gannett (b. 1923)
Illustrated by Ruth Chrisman Gannett (1896–1979)
Published in 1948 by Random House
Newbery Honor Book
Ages 7 to 9   88 pages

In a fanciful book, nine-year-old Elmer Elevator travels to distant Wild Island to free a baby dragon enslaved by wild animals. Using both ingenuity and the extensive contents of his backpack (which includes lollipops, hair ribbons, and chewing gum), Elmer outwits the captors. In a series of hilarious incidents, Elmer meets some impressive animals along the way — including a tiger, gorilla, lion, rhinoceros, and crocodile.

Sometimes children's books come about because of long, deliberate planning. But sometimes, like Minerva, they arrive fully grown. *My Father's Dragon* emerged from a two-week vacation.

A graduate of Vassar College, Ruth Stiles Gannett worked as a technician in medical research. Eventually, she took a job at a ski lodge in Vermont, but because of the seasonal nature of the work she returned to her father's Connecticut home to hunt for employment. As entertainment during two long, rainy weeks, she wrote the first draft of *My Father's Dragon* with no thought of publication. Her stepmother, Ruth Chrisman Gannett, who had previously illustrated a Caldecott Honor Book and a Newbery Medal winner, was particularly adept at drawing animals both realistic and yet filled with character. She created vigorous black-and-white line drawings for her stepdaughter's book. Peter Kahn — an artist, printer, and designer — helped his future wife, Ruth Stiles Gannett, with the maps of Tangerina and Wild Island, the design of the book, and the choice of type. So the entire project became a family affair.

Winning both the *New York Herald Tribune* Children's Book Festival Award and a Newbery Honor, the book found immediate recognition and an enthusiastic audience. Although Gannett wrote two sequels — *Elmer and the Dragon* and *The Dragons of Blueland* — essentially she pursued other interests. She raised seven daughters and worked in an elementary school. But she spent one very fruitful respite creating a classic book for children.

Stone Fox

....

Written by John Reynolds Gardiner (b. 1944)
Illustrated by Marcia Sewall (b. 1935)
Published in 1980 by Harper & Row
Ages 7 to 9   83 pages

Of all the authors and illustrators in this book, the least likely candidate for inclusion is John Reynolds Gardiner. As a boy, he rebelled — whatever his parents wanted him to do, he did exactly the opposite. So when they wanted him to read, he didn't. In fact, he did not read his first novel until the age of nineteen. As a nonreader, he had problems with grammar and spelling. At UCLA he entered the lowest-level English class, along with foreign students who couldn't speak English but proved superior to Gardiner in writing.

However, Gardiner, an engineer who went on to work at McDonnell Douglas Corporation, exhibited great creativity; he even patented a plastic necktie filled with water and goldfish. Encouraged by his brother, who recognized his original mind, Gardiner took a television-writing class and later worked for Martin Tahse, who was designing "After School Specials" for television.

The editor Barbara Fenton, intrigued by Tahse's work, sent him a query letter, asking if he had a book that he wanted to write. He had no such book but sent instead a television treatment of a story written by John Gardiner. Although Fenton didn't know if Gardiner could flesh out and expand the idea, she asked him to write a first and last chapter, to see if he could create fiction from his compelling story line.

Based on a Rocky Mountain legend, *Stone Fox* contains every element of character and plot possible in such a slim volume. Two protagonists, Willy, a boy who wants to save his grandfather's farm, and a Native American, Stone Fox, trying to buy back his tribe's land, compete for prize money in the National Dogsled Race. Told simply and directly, the story raises issues about the plight of Native Americans and also speaks about love, loyalty, and the sacrifice of Willy's true friend, Searchlight the dog.

An adroit combination of adventure, sports, Western, and dog story, *Stone Fox* rarely fails to captivate young readers. In fact, it often emerges as the favorite of young boys in these years. This book written by a reading rebel can quickly convince other reading rebels that they might actually enjoy the story and characters that lie between two covers.

Snow-White and the Seven Dwarfs
....

Written by Jacob (1785–1863) and Wilhelm (1786–1859) Grimm
Translated by Randall Jarrell (1914–1965)
Illustrated by Nancy Ekholm Burkert (b. 1933)
Published in 1972 by Michael di Capua/Farrar, Straus and Giroux
Caldecott Honor Book
Ages 7 to 9   32 pages

Having created a book she wanted to publish, the artist Nancy Ekholm Burkert decided she would submit her effort to her top five publishers. One of these, Alfred A. Knopf, tentatively accepted the book. But while she was revising it, they offered her Roald Dahl's *James and the Giant Peach* to illustrate. Although her first effort never got published, her illustrations for Dahl, and a handful of picture books, helped establish her as one of the finest American artists creating books for children today.

The most accomplished of these books, *Snow-White and the Seven Dwarfs*, brings new life and vitality to the well-known story of Snow-White, an innocent girl threatened by an evil stepmother and befriended by dwarfs. The poet Randall Jarrell's translation goes back to the original Grimms, who collected folktales of the people, not tales for children. Jarrell avoids none of the grisly details: the stepmother eats what she believes to be Snow-White's liver and heart, and she dances to her death in red-hot slippers. The original tale contains many dark and disturbing moments, and Burkert illustrates them accordingly.

Burkert took three years to complete her research for the book, visiting Germany's Black Forest, the Cluny Museum in Paris, and the Cloisters in New York. In the illustration of the wicked queen making poison, Burkert created a setting where everything in the room was noxious. Burkert's twelve-year-old daughter, Clare, served as the model for Snow-White. The artwork, using brush and colored ink, is marked by its flow, vitality, delicacy, and rhythm. Like the illuminators of manuscripts in the Middle Ages, Burkert works with awe-inspiring precision. She has always been drawn to the Flemish masters of the fifteenth century, and she paid her homage to them in this book.

Including the most breathtaking illustrations ever prepared for a fairy tale, the book serves as an antidote to the saccharine images of the Walt Disney film. Any child or adult who wants to comprehend the true meaning of folklore will want to spend a great deal of time studying both Randall Jarrell's translation and Nancy Ekholm Burkert's luminescent illustrations.

Misty of Chincoteague

Written by Marguerite Henry (1902–1997)
Illustrated by Wesley Dennis (1903–1966)
Published in 1947 by Rand McNally
Newbery Honor Book
Ages 7 to 9   176 pages

In this book, Maureen and Paul Beebe, residents of Chincoteague Island off the coast of Virginia, long to own one of the wild horses of nearby Assateague Island; legend claims that these animals were the descendants of a stallion named Fire Chief and his mares from a Spanish ship that went down in a gale. Every year some of the Assateague horses are captured and sold on Pony Penning Day. With long planning and great effort, the Beebe children raise the money to buy Phantom and her colt Misty; eventually the mare escapes, but Misty stays with the family.

While researching *Misty of Chincoteague*, Marguerite Henry traveled with the illustrator Wesley Dennis to Chincoteague Island on Pony Penning Day. There she visited the Beebe Ranch and talked to Maureen and Paul, who helped care for their grandfather's ponies. As Henry looked over the ponies, she saw one she desperately wanted for her own — a creature marked with what resembled a white map of America on her coat. Realizing that this pony would be critical for her book, Henry bargained with the grandfather, promising to make Maureen and Paul characters in her story and eventually to return Misty to the Beebe family.

But because the colt was still very young, Henry left it with her mother, Phantom, and promised $150 to Mr. Beebe, who agreed to ship the pony to Henry later. After Mr. Beebe studied Wesley Dennis's sketches, he said, "Feller, I can eenamost hear your picture-horses whinnerin' and buglin' . . . Yup, I've done the right thing, fer sure."

But when Misty arrived at Henry's home in Illinois by train, she looked very different from the horse Henry had seen. In fact, Henry even initially accused Grandfather Beebe of being a horse trader — for there were no markings, no palomino coat, no white map of America. A sooty gray, Misty looked woolly rather than sleek. In fact, Henry's husband thought she resembled a Siberian goat. But as winter turned into spring, Misty grew slimmer and trimmer; she eventually shed her winter coat and became the pony Henry remembered.

Misty took up residence in the Henry household; she even came into the living room and studio. She posed with children and visited schools, libraries, and book shows. In a moment of triumph, Misty attended the annual American Library Association conference in Grand Rapids, Michigan, as an honorary member of the ALA. Eventually, Henry kept her promise to Grandfather Beebe to send Misty back to Chincoteague to have a colt. The children of

America named the baby Phantom Wings, and Misty had other foals, Wisp O'Mist and Stormy. At the age of twenty-six, Misty died in her sleep at her home in Chincoteague.

Henry has been justifiably praised over the years for her ability to write compelling horse stories. She thoroughly researched each book, paying detailed and specific attention to every illustration. Not only did she show Wesley Dennis where each drawing should appear in the text, she provided him with photographs, clippings, and visual materials to use for his final work — everything from pictures of pony parades in Ireland to one of the real Fire Chief of Chincoteague.

In January 1990, the Misty of Chincoteague Foundation was established to preserve the last piece of the original Beebe Ranch and the original open land on Chincoteague Island. Today thousands of visitors go to Chincoteague Island, to see the country that Misty roamed. A story about the human capacity for unselfishness, a story about the history of these islands, and a story about the fantasy of almost every child — owning a horse — *Misty of Chincoteague* has taken on a life of its own, well beyond the horse that inspired it and its creator.

Babe: The Gallant Pig

Written by Dick King-Smith (b. 1922)
Illustrated by Mary Rayner (b. 1933)
Published in 1985 by Alfred A. Knopf
Ages 7 to 9   118 pages

Like *Charlotte's Web*, the plot of *Babe: The Gallant Pig* began in the author's mind as a way to save a pig's life. While manning the "Guess the Weight of the Pig" stall in an English village summer fête, Dick King-Smith thought about the contest's result: the winner would probably kill the pig for food. He began to ruminate on this problem in search of an alternative. What if the pig could live on a farm with a sheep dog as a foster mom? Suppose the pig wanted to follow in her footsteps? Although he couldn't be a sheep dog, he could become a sheep pig.

With this sequence of events, King-Smith outlined the tale of an orphan pig, Babe, adopted by a farmer and his sheep dog. By virtue of intelligence, courage, and determination — and particularly politeness — Babe wins the Grand Challenge Sheep-dog Trials.

Dick King-Smith came to children's book writing after a series of careers — soldier, farmer, salesman, factory worker, and teacher. His emotionally rewarding but financially dubious stint as a farmer provided most of his insights for the book. He loved working with pigs and had particularly fond memories of raising a six-hundred-pound porker called Monty. When King-Smith came to write for children in his late fifties, while teaching school, all of his life experiences became fodder for his books. Although he wrote animal fantasies, his books have a thorough grounding in the realities of farm life, and they all testify to his love of animals.

Originally called *The Sheep-Pig* when published in England, *Babe: The Gallant Pig* appeared to a flock of rave reviews in the United States. For a decade it was one of those lesser-known titles that children's book enthusiasts loved to promote and was made famous by a movie in 1995. Now with more than a hundred children's books in print, Dick King-Smith has been as popular with young readers as he has been prolific. But of all his titles, *Babe: The Gallant Pig* has proved the most enduring, a testament to the intelligence and winning ways of this common farm animal.

Betsy-Tacy

Written by Maud Hart Lovelace (1892–1980)
Illustrated by Lois Lenski (1893–1974)
Published in 1940 by T. Y. Crowell
Ages 7 to 9   132 pages

Although written as fiction, the Betsy-Tacy books present an autobiographical account of Maud Hart Lovelace's own life and her days growing up in Mankato, Minnesota. A writer from an early age, she once asked her mother, "How do you spell going down the street?" As a child she kept scrapbooks and diaries; later she drew upon these tools to write the Betsy-Tacy stories. At first Lovelace wrote historical novels for adults, but with the birth of her daughter, Merian, she began telling bedtime stories about her childhood in Mankato. For Merian, she recounted the events of her childhood and her red-haired best friend, Bick Kenney, whom Lovelace met at her fifth birthday party.

When a new family moves into Betsy's neighborhood, she gets her wish for a girlfriend her age. In fact, she and Tacy become such good friends that everyone thinks of them as one person, Betsy-Tacy. Depicting a secure childhood, a loving family, and a very special and enduring friendship between two little girls, *Betsy-Tacy* deals with real childhood tragedy and the way that children cope with death, when Tacy's baby brother dies. Subsequent books followed, taking the girls through high school, college, and marriage.

Lovelace submitted *Betsy-Tacy* to a publisher's children's book contest, but it failed to win. She then became a client of the New York literary agent Nannine Joseph, who also represented the illustrator Lois Lenski. Joseph asked Lenski to prepare illustrations for the book, and Lenski then brought the book to her longtime friend, the editor Elizabeth Riley. In 1940 the first of the ten-book Betsy-Tacy series appeared.

Although the books went out of print for a number of years, Betsy-Tacy fans managed to get them reissued. Both the Betsy-Tacy Society and the Maud Hart Lovelace Society contain legions of readers who adored these books as children. Beloved by generations, these gentle, old-fashioned stories present a simpler, kinder era, almost a century ago — when children were mischievous but not troubled, and when families and friendship defined the life of a community.

Sarah, Plain and Tall

··

By Patricia MacLachlan (b. 1938)
Published in 1985 by Charlotte Zolotow/Harper & Row
Newbery Medal
Ages 7 to 9   64 pages

Sarah, Plain and Tall began as a journey. As Patricia MacLachlan traveled with her three children to North Dakota, she was able to show them the farm where her father had been born in a sod house and a landscape that they had never seen. Later as she worked on a book featuring a prairie setting, MacLachlan preserved a story her mother had passed on to her about one of their ancestors who had married a mail-order bride. That bride had haunted, nagged, and begged MacLachlan to tell the story for years, ever since MacLachlan had first introduced her in *Arthur, for the Very First Time.*

As MacLachlan's mother succumbed to Alzheimer's disease, MacLachlan worked to preserve this ancestor's story as well as her mother's history. One day, when her mother still was functioning, they went for a drive in the country. Suddenly her mother reached over to her to say, "Now, who are you?" "I am your daughter," MacLachlan answered. "Ah, then isn't it nice that I like you" came the reply. With this emotional background, *Sarah, Plain and Tall* emerged as a celebration of family and the beauty of human relationships.

In a spare tale, set in the nineteenth century, a young girl, Anna, tells the story of her father, Jacob Witting, a poor farmer, and his newspaper ad to secure a wife for himself and a mother for his children. After a series of letters, Sarah Wheaton leaves her home in Maine to join this prairie family. Told in a terse, evocative style, with careful use of words and imagery, the novel exhibits a depth of feeling and characterization that surpasses its brevity. MacLachlan weaves a heartwarming story about how a family forms even when the members are not related by blood.

Since its publication, *Sarah, Plain and Tall* has become a favorite in the classroom, in mother-daughter book groups, and at family reading time. After being adapted for a Hallmark Hall of Fame television special featuring Glenn Close as Sarah, the book reached an even wider audience. For millions of children, the simple letter from Sarah to Jacob has become part of their literary heritage: "I will come by train. I will wear a yellow bonnet. I am plain and tall. Tell them I sing."

The New Kid on the Block

Written by Jack Prelutsky (b. 1940)
Illustrated by James Stevenson (b. 1929)
Published in 1984 by Greenwillow Books
Ages 7 to 9   160 pages

When children view poetry as boring, *The New Kid on the Block* changes their minds. Few dog lovers, for instance, can resist these lines: "My dog, he is a stupid dog, / his mind is slow and thick, / he's never learned to catch a ball, / he cannot fetch a stick. / My dog, he is a greedy dog, / he eats enough for three, / his belly bulges to the ground, / he is the dog for me."

The author of these verses, Jack Prelutsky, actually wanted to be an illustrator. But he also made up poems to go along with his art. When the editor Susan Hirschman saw his work, although she loved the writing she knew the drawing had to go. In his early years as a writer, Prelutsky drove a taxi and was often impoverished and literally starving. So if he delivered a poem to Hirschman, she would take him to lunch in Macmillan's executive dining room. Twenty years after their first meeting and many lunches later, Jack Prelutsky wrote 107 poems for this book, featuring such unforgettable creatures as the Slyne, the gloopy Gloppers, and Baloney Belly Billy.

In 1976, Hirschman, who had known James Stevenson's *New*

Yorker cartoons, saw some of his picture-book dummies. Shy and retiring, Stevenson, quite unlike Prelutsky, never wanted to meet with his editor over lunch or anyplace else. At first he declined to illustrate this collection of verses. Eventually he agreed on Hirschman's insistence to take a second look and created the lighthearted and joyous art that perfectly balances the bite in these poems.

This fortunate collaboration resulted in one of the most popular poetry collections of all time for children. Once hooked on the poetry in this volume, children can go on to read other Prelutsky-Stevenson volumes and other poetry, with the assurance that it will be appealing. Wallace Stegner believed that the purpose of poetry was to contribute to man's happiness. Few poetry books have ever created as much happiness for its readers as *The New Kid on the Block*.

Grandfather's Journey

By Allen Say (b. 1937)
Published in 1993 by Houghton Mifflin
Caldecott Medal
Ages 7 to 9   32 pages

Born in Yokohama, Allen Say apprenticed himself at the age of twelve to a famous Japanese cartoonist before he immigrated to the United States. At first Say hated his new country; thrown into military school in California, he found himself quite unhappy with both his family and his new surroundings. But many years later, while working on this book about his grandfather, he began to identify more with him. And when he wrote "After a time, I came to love the land my grandfather had loved," Say realized that he had come to terms with his own feelings and experiences as an immigrant.

In this autobiographical picture book, a young Japanese man sets off to see the world. In a photo album of exquisite images, he explores North America and eventually brings his Japanese bride to California. Returning to Japan, Say's grandfather experiences World War II and the devastation of his home. In time, his grandson leaves Japan to live in California.

Unlike many illustrators, who need a finished story line before they begin their art, Say executed all of the illustrations first and then wrote the text to follow. For *Grandfather's Journey* he took two years to create the delicate watercolor art, marked by intense colors. Reproducing that art, and keeping the colors clean and pure, proved extremely difficult; the publisher rejected three attempts to print the book. Finally, Walter Lorraine, the editor; Donna McCarthy, the production manager; and Say decided on an innovative but effective production technique that helped capture the vibrancy of the colors. In the end, the art looks luminous, just as Say intended in his original illustrations.

Because America is a nation of immigrants, *Grandfather's Journey* tells the story of all of our citizens. The lines "But I also miss the mountains and rivers of my childhood. I miss my old friends . . . the moment I am in one country, I am homesick for the other" speak to many readers from different immigrant backgrounds or those who have simply lived in two different places.

Little House in the Big Woods

Written by Laura Ingalls Wilder (1867–1957)
Illustrated by Garth Williams (1912–1996)
Published in 1932 by Harper Brothers
Ages 7 to 9   238 pages

In a story about family devotion, hard work, and struggle against adversity, Laura Ingalls and her mother, father, and sister Mary demonstrate all the virtues of the pioneer settlers in the Wisconsin woods in 1870. They hunt and trap, make cheese and maple sugar, but they also sing, dance, and enjoy life. With a high degree of literary panache, the Little House novels, a series of nine books, show the pioneer migration of the Wilder family from Lake Pepin,

Wisconsin, to De Smet, South Dakota, about three hundred miles away.

Even by 1932, when it was published, *Little House in the Big Woods* captured a simpler time in America's history. Today it can fill readers with a powerful sense of longing for an era long gone by. Although, on occasion, unfortunately marred by the racial prejudices of its day, the narrative gives children a sense of being snugly tucked into a cabin in the woods while the wind howls around them.

Great books often involve extensive collaboration — usually on the part of an author or editor, sometimes on the part of an illustrator and author. But in the case of the Little House books, the collaboration appears to have been between Laura Ingalls Wilder and her daughter Rose Wilder Lane, a story only recently told in a biography of Rose Wilder Lane by William Holtz, *Ghost in the Little House*.

Laura Ingalls Wilder, who had spent her childhood on the American frontier, had thought about writing the story of her life for over twenty years, but she did not begin doing so until her sixties. In about 1930 she finished a factual, first-person narrative, her autobiography. Working with the material, Rose Wilder Lane, an accomplished writer and novelist who had ghostwritten many books in her lifetime, crafted a hundred-page manuscript called "Pioneer Girl." She then prepared a twenty-page third-person narrative, "When Grandma Was a Little Girl," that she and her mother saw as picture-book text. They sent that book to a children's editor at Knopf, Marian Fiery. Fiery, however, wanted the book expanded to 25,000 words and filled with details of pioneer life. Rose instructed her mother, "If you find it easier to write in the first person, write that way. I will change it into the third person later." Eventually the two produced a manuscript that Fiery now called "Little House in the Woods."

After the manuscript was finished, Fiery lost her job at Knopf but had such faith in the book that she passed it on to her friend at Harper Brothers, Virginia Kirkus. All editors should have such friends! Kirkus began reading the manuscript on a late train home to Westport, Connecticut, and missed her stop, so involved had she become in her reading. Accepting the manuscript for publication at the height of the Depression, she knew she had found "that miracle book that no depression could stop." The Little House books found an immediate audience and sold very well. By 1936, Laura Ingalls Wilder was making $800 annually in royalty payments, quite an impressive sum at the time.

From the extant manuscripts, the collaboration of mother and daughter can be clearly detailed. Wilder provided the raw data, the information, the vantage point; Lane transformed it all into fiction, with subtlety, shading, character, and nuance. Although only Laura Ingalls Wilder received credit for the books, in today's publishing environment undoubtedly both names would grace the title page.

In 1953, Garth Williams illustrated new editions of the Little House saga, and his drawings have become synonymous with the books themselves. These reissues revitalized the series, and eventually a television drama would create an even greater audience. Today these books stand as the most important American historical novels for children about the last half of the nineteenth century — and as one of the greatest mother-daughter collaborations of all time.

Books for Middle Readers

Ages 8 to 11

The Secret Garden

Written by Frances Hodgson Burnett (1849–1924)
Illustrated by Tasha Tudor (b. 1915)
Published in 1911 by Frederick Stokes
Ages 8 to 11   358 pages

Sometimes the passion of a writer or the writer's country can influence its greatest books. Books such as *Charlotte's Web* can be seen as the manifestation of the American love of the farm and country, translated into a book for children. Hence, it is not surprising that the English, who love to cultivate "a bit of earth," wrote the two great children's books with a garden setting, *The Secret Garden* and *Tom's Midnight Garden* (see page 120).

When Frances Hodgson Burnett created *The Secret Garden*, she lived on Long Island, New York, far away from her childhood home of Manchester, England, and the beloved gardens in her adult home of Maytham Hall, Kent. At Maytham, she had discovered a long-neglected garden, where she pruned bushes, trimmed trees, and cleared weeds and thorns. In a year, she turned this garden, which had been enclosed by brick walls in 1721, into a rose garden and planted it with three hundred rosebushes.

Today *The Secret Garden* seems an almost nostalgic reminder of a somehow sweeter era. But in its time, the book presented modern protagonists — the hero, Colin Craven, and the heroine, Mary Lennox — who quickly emerge as thoroughly unattractive children. In the process of the story, however, the spoiled orphan Mary experiences a transformation as she and Colin, and the robin Dickon, work in a languishing garden. Not only does the garden revive, but so do the children. Unlike other books of the early 1900s, *The Secret Garden* suggests that children should be self-reliant, have faith in themselves, and listen to their own conscience.

Francis Hodgson Burnett excelled in the telling detail. You can learn the elements of pruning roses from *The Secret Garden*, and the book contains many other accurate and detailed descriptions. "It is not enough to mention they have tea," she once said, "you must specify the muffins."

First serialized in *American Magazine,* the story appeared under the title "Mistress Mary." It sold out its first edition even before publication and was widely read by adult fans of Burnett's earlier books, but it achieved little notoriety during the author's life. Throughout that life, Burnett received both fame and fortune as the author of *Little Lord Fauntleroy,* her most popular book. In fact, her *New York Times* obituary never even mentioned *The Secret Garden.* But like the roses that lay dormant in the walled garden, this book has flourished with each passing year. Gardening and children's book enthusiasts for almost a century have identified with Mary Lennox's plea, "Might I have a bit of earth?"

The Incredible Journey

Written by Sheila Burnford (1918–1984)
Illustrated by Carl Burger (1888–1967)
Published in 1961 by Atlantic Monthly Press
Ages 8 to 11   145 pages

Editors often become aware of the controversies surrounding books only after they have been published. But in the case of some books, the most heated debates happen even before the manuscript is accepted by a publishing house.

When *The Incredible Journey* landed on the desk of Emilie McLeod, children's book publisher of the Atlantic Monthly Press, she instantly knew she wanted to publish it. But in those days, Atlantic had a financial arrangement with Little, Brown and Company, and McLeod needed to obtain permission to proceed from its children's book publisher, Helen Jones. Jones shared none of her colleague's enthusiasm for the book and refused to take the project on. Both women of distinct yet different tastes, the two became embroiled in a heated controversy over the book — neither willing to back down. Eventually the higher levels of management became involved in trying to quell this donnybrook. Finally, the publisher of Atlantic's adult list agreed to take the book on, and his counterpart at Little, Brown gave permission. Consequently, one of the greatest books for children from the 1960s first saw the light of day on an adult list, even though no one considered it an adult book.

In *The Incredible Journey,* three animal friends — an old bull terrier, a Siamese cat, and a Labrador retriever — attempt a treacherous 250-mile journey through the Canadian wilderness. When their owners go on vacation, the trio are left in the care of a family friend, but they escape to embark on their trip home. During the journey, they struggle against wild animals, unsympathetic humans, and the rugged landscape.

Burnford based these three characters on her own three pets. When Bill, the bull terrier, died, she wrote the novel, using her observations about communication between her cat and dogs. Unlike many books of this genre — *Sounder, Where the Red Fern Grows,* and *Old Yeller* — the animals remain alive throughout the narrative. With a happy ending and lots of adventure, the book satisfies the craving of children who want a compelling animal story that leaves them smiling.

The Dark Is Rising

....

By Susan Cooper (b. 1935)
Published in 1973 by Margaret K. McElderry/Atheneum Publishers
Newbery Honor Book
Ages 8 to 11   244 pages

An Oxford University graduate and journalist, Susan Cooper married an American and for years found herself homesick for Britain. So she turned to the folklore, fairy tale, and myth of her childhood, notably Arthurian legend, for the material in *The Dark Is Rising.* Not only did she recreate the setting, Buckinghamshire, England, where she grew up, from a distance, but the ice and cold that permeate the book emerged while she sat in her bathing suit, with her back to the Caribbean Sea, a small lizard standing on her typewriter.

Susan Cooper's first book, *Over Sea, Under Stone,* had been written for a publisher's family-adventure story competition. In that book, Cooper featured a character named Merriman Lyon, based on the Merlin of Arthurian legend and on her grandfather, a man with a noble nose and bushy white hair. In her new manuscript, she wanted to develop Merriman and his ideas about good and evil more thoroughly; Cooper formed her own images of the dark and light during her World War II childhood, when England came under Hitler's attack.

The Dark Is Rising introduces the character of Will Stanton. On his eleventh birthday on December 21, Will learns that he is the last of the Old Ones and must join together six signs — wood, bronze, iron, water, fire, and stone. Will's special powers come at a cost: "Any great gift or talent is a burden . . . and you will often long to be free of it. If you were born with the gift then you must serve it."

Many readers enjoy *The Dark Is Rising* as the winter solstice approaches and the days get shorter. But the novel serves as a fantasy for all seasons. With its understanding of the universal struggle of good and evil, and its underlying theme of how children grow into adults, *The Dark Is Rising* proves to be a book young readers remember, with great passion, well into their adult years.

The BFG

....

Written by Roald Dahl (1916–1990)
Illustrated by Quentin Blake (b. 1932)
Published in 1982 by Farrar, Straus and Giroux
Ages 8 to 11   208 pages

Roald Dahl's books frequently began in other books he wrote. In the second chapter of *Danny, the Champion of the World,*

Danny's father tells his son a series of bedtime stories "about an enormous fellow called The Big Friendly Giant, or the BFG for short."

The BFG, a likable giant, devotes his life to collecting and administering dreams. His sensitive hearing enables him to detect their sounds as they buzz through the air. And after he abducts Sophie, an orphan, the two of them develop a plan to rid the country of other, pestilent giants.

The editor of *The BFG,* Stephen Roxburgh, proved to be one of Dahl's most exacting editors. He spent days drafting his editorial suggestions to Dahl, ten typed, single-spaced pages that commented on inconsistencies, clichés, and matters of taste. Dahl told Roxburgh that he was "absolutely swishboggled and sloshbunkled" by the trouble the editor had taken with his work. He accepted these criticisms, greatly improving the manuscript. *The BFG* remains Dahl's most critically successful work, an example of the author's broad genius and the editor's insights combining felicitously to produce a classic.

Dahl and Quentin Blake worked with the same attention to the drawings, with Dahl sometimes altering the text to accommodate Blake's artwork. Ambidextrous, Blake drew the art for the book with pens in both hands.

Sometimes life imitates fiction. In *The BFG,* the giant goes to Buckingham Palace, where he blows a dream through the queen's bedroom window. When the queen awakes, she finds Sophie on the windowsill. In July 1982, after the book had been written but before its publication, Queen Elizabeth II woke up in Buckingham Palace to find a man in her bedroom. The real-life intruder, however, found himself whisked away by security guards.

Dahl and all his books have frequently met with adult criticism — but seldom has a discouraging word even been whispered by the under-twelve set. They remain enchanted by Dahl's trademarks as a writer — inventive wordplay, amiable children, nasty villains, lots of action, and a large dose of nonsense. And, of course, unforgettable characters such as the Big Friendly Giant.

Because of Winn-Dixie

....

By Kate DiCamillo (b. 1964)
Published in 2000 by Candlewick Press
Newbery Honor Book
Ages 8 to 11   182 pages

Written in a beautiful and simple cadence, *Because of Winn-Dixie* presents the healing power of a stray mutt, Winn-Dixie, a dog with a lot of personality and a charismatic smile. Named after the store in which he was found in Naomi, Florida, Winn-Dixie takes over the lives of two people, a preacher and a young girl, ten-year-old Opal. Abandoned by their wife and mother, the two have maintained a marginal existence, but Winn-Dixie changes the family dynamic and helps widen their circle of friends. This gentle book about people coming together to combat loneliness and heartache — with a little canine assistance — features a quirky heroine, memorable characters, and an assured Southern voice.

For years, Kate DiCamillo tried unsuccessfully to get her writing published. Rejected by several publishers, the manuscript for *Because of Winn-Dixie* languished in the offices of Candlewick Press for several months. Finally a young editorial assistant, Kara LaReau, brought it to the attention of the editor Liz Bicknell. Bicknell laughed when she read the first chapter and then cried; after finishing it, she believed it to be one of the best middle-grade novels she'd ever seen. After a couple of calls to the author, unreturned, Bicknell finally reached DiCamillo. No doubt surprised to hear from Candlewick so long after submitting the book, the author said simply, "I need to take a bath." However, the next day she called back, and they agreed on a publishing plan for *Because of Winn-Dixie*.

Believing very strongly in this book by a new author, Candlewick printed a few chapters in the center of its catalog; after that, the book caught on by word of mouth. Although published in this century, *Because of Winn-Dixie* possesses all the qualities of a children's classic. Winning a Newbery Honor, the book has also received countless awards chosen by children. One child said, "If *Winn-Dixie* weren't a book, I'd marry it." Although they can't marry *Winn-Dixie*, many children and adults have grown to love and cherish this heartwarming story.

Half Magic
....

Written by Edward Eager (1911–1964)
Illustrated by N. M. Bodecker (1922–1988)
Published in 1954 by Harcourt Brace
Ages 8 to 11   192 pages

While attending Harvard College, Edward Eager wrote a play that proved so successful that he left school to pursue writing plays and songs for the theater, radio, and television. After he had a young son, he began reading the fantasy books of the English writer E. Nesbit, which until then had been unknown to Eager. Inspired by them, Eager decided to write a fantasy in Nesbit's tradition, and he acknowledges her in each of his books so that his readers might be led back to her work.

In seven books, Eager wrote about "daily magic" — integrating the realism of ordinary children with romantic adventures that come about because of the sudden appearance of a magic object. All of these books possess a totally childlike understanding of magic. In *Half Magic,* four siblings find a talisman that grants their wishes — but only in part. Because this kind of magic can get one into trouble and has its own rules, they experience a series of mishaps: Martha, for instance, wishes for the cat to talk, and the semiarticulate feline engages in a flow of half-meaningless words. Although the children experience a great deal of excitement to enliven their dull summer, in the end they decide to pass on their charm to two small children in another part of town.

Although not universally praised by critics, who often preferred the works of E. Nesbit, the book appealed immensely to children — who can easily comprehend the book's premise. The reasons for Eager's popularity with his audience have not changed for fifty years: he wrote accessible, plot-driven fantasy with a good deal of humor and inventiveness. His strong characters and lively dialogue, sharpened by his playwriting experience, keep readers thoroughly engaged. In more recent years, while E. Nesbit's audience has waned in the United States, Eager's novels have found a more avid reception — now fueled by the recent fantasy converts of the Harry Potter books.

Harriet the Spy

Written by Louise Fitzhugh (1928–1974)
Published in 1964 by Harper & Row
Ages 8 to 11   300 pages

I want to know everything, everything. . . . Everything in the world," cries the privileged, eleven-year-old Harriet M. Welsch, who always carries a notebook and records her observations. Harriet dresses like a spy in a dark hooded sweatshirt and old blue jeans, with a flashlight, knife, and spare pens hanging from hooks on her belt. She eavesdrops in dumbwaiters; she listens through doors. She is even willing to take dancing lessons because the famous spy Mata Hari knew how to dance.

While under the care of Ole Golly, her nurse, Harriet manages to keep her spying life in order. But after Ole Golly leaves to get married, Harriet's notebook ends up in the hands of her classmates and her activities begin to spiral out of control. As a protagonist, Harriet incorporates all the pain, loneliness, curiosity, and excitement of childhood. Angry, an outsider, she tentatively finds a way to connect herself to others. But no one believes at the end of the novel that Harriet has changed all that much. As she writes in her notebook, "NOW THAT THINGS ARE BACK TO NORMAL, I CAN GET SOME REAL WORK DONE."

Although she created the quintessential New York child, Louise Fitzhugh began her life as the quintessential Southerner in a gothic family that might have been created by Tennessee Williams or William Faulkner. She wrote a few other books in her lifetime but primarily viewed herself as an artist. She sketched the way Harriet took notes — constantly, without censor.

Harriet the Spy arrived at the publisher as a manuscript containing only Harriet's comments on her spy route. The editors Ursula Nordstrom and Charlotte Zolotow elicited the book from Fitzhugh using the Socratic method. They asked questions such as "Why was Harriet angry?" "Why was she keeping a diary?" With every new query, Fitzhugh sent in a chapter of the book. Writing *Harriet the Spy* was like playing a game.

Upon publication, *Harriet the Spy* received some scathing reviews. The editor of *The Horn Book Magazine* wrote: "Children, however, do not enjoy cynicism. I doubt its appeal to many of them." Harriet was also called "one of the most fatiguing, ill-mannered children imaginable." But children, identifying with Harriet, read and loved the book. In the late 1960s, Harriet the Spy Clubs became the rage, and young fans hid under tables in schools across the country, taking notes. The success of this fresh and frank novel influenced the children's books of that decade, brining them with a new wave of realism.

Children today can easily trace the locations in the book, close to Fitzhugh's East 85th Street apartment, and it's possible to take a walking tour of Harriet's neighborhood by consulting Leonard S. Marcus's *Storied City* or going to www.purple-socks.com/places .htm. Be sure to bring a notebook!

Humbug Mountain

··

Written by Sid Fleischman (b. 1920)
Illustrated by Eric Von Schmidt (b. 1931)
Published in 1978 by Atlantic Monthly Press
Ages 8 to 11   133 pages

Narrated by Wiley, the son of an itinerant newspaperman, *Humbug Mountain* incorporates a great deal of American tall-tale humor. It features the Flint family, down on their luck and roaming the West to look for Grandpa. In the process, they find a haunted riverboat, start a gold rush, and discover a petrified man. Sid Fleischman manages to combine history and adventure, a fast-paced plot, and the essence of a Western novel in a text that reads aloud beautifully.

Fleischman came to writing children's books after many years of seemingly unrelated experiences. In his entertaining autobiography, *The Abracadabra Kid: A Writer's Life,* he details his humble beginnings as a magician. As a child, his sheer joy in being able to execute card tricks or conjure rabbits out of hats caused him to read books about magic; write a book about magic, *Between Cocktails;* travel the country in a vaudeville show; and eventually finance his college education by publishing magic tricks. Along the way, he learned to print advertising flyers and worked for newspapers.

Although Fleischman pursued a successful career as an adult screenwriter in Hollywood, he began creating children's books for his own three children. He sent his first book, *Mr. Mysterious and Company,* off to his agent, saying only, "I seem to have written a children's book. If you don't care to read it, I will understand. Drop it into the wastebasket." Instead the agent sent it to the editor Emilie McLeod, who made an offer the next morning, launching Fleischman's new career. One day while signing books at the Santa Monica, California, library, he looked up and saw his youngest daughter standing in line.

Winner of the Newbery Medal for *The Whipping Boy,* Fleischman experienced another triumph when his son, Paul, also won the Newbery Medal for *Joyful Noise;* to date, they remain the only father-son combination to receive this prestigious award.

Lincoln: A Photobiography

....

By Russell Freedman (b. 1929)
Published in 1987 by Clarion Books
Newbery Medal
Ages 8 to 11   150 pages

Born in San Francisco, Russell Freedman grew up in an ideal environment for a future writer. His parents actually met in a bookshop, where his mother worked as a clerk; his father served as the West Coast sales representative for Macmillan Publishers. So John Steinbeck and Margaret Mitchell, who wrote *Gone With the Wind,* actually came to dinner, and Freedman found himself surrounded by books and book people.

Russell Freedman created thirty-three books, many of them about natural science, before he turned his hand to writing a biography about Abraham Lincoln, his boyhood hero. As a child, he had thought of Lincoln as uncomplicated, but when he came across a quotation describing Lincoln as "the most secretive — reticent — shut-mouthed man that ever lived," he began to explore the man more thoroughly.

A master researcher, Freedman visited the sites he went on to write about, studied Lincoln's handwriting, and became totally engaged by his subject. The resulting book exhibits his passion and enthusiasm — but stays grounded in exacting research and writing standards. Freedman invented no dialogue for the book: "Lincoln didn't need a speechwriter and he doesn't need one now." With graceful prose, Freedman tells a story so compelling that many readers cry upon reading about Lincoln's assassination even though they already know about it.

But the book transcends biography and also paints a wider political canvas. "My biography of Abraham Lincoln tells the story of an ambitious, self-educated man who goes from a log cabin to the White House, but at the same time it's also a story about slavery, racism, class privilege, and economic and political forces."

Not only did *Lincoln* receive much critical acclaim, it won the Newbery Medal, something an information book had not done for thirty-two years. After its publication, the book brought renewed focus and attention to information books by writers and publishers; in fact, it has become the standard of excellence for all contemporary children's biographies.

In an age when children need heroes and heroines, Russell Freedman writes about his own and makes nonfiction pleasurable to read. Freedman also maintains an ironic and charming sense of humor about his work. His favorite letter from a child about *Lincoln* reads simply, "Did you take the photographs yourself?"

Julie of the Wolves

Written by Jean Craighead George (b. 1919)
Illustrated by John Schoenherr (b. 1935)
Published in 1972 by Harper & Row
Newbery Medal
Ages 8 to 11   170 pages

The daughter of two entomologists, Jean Craighead George grew up in a family of naturalists. When she got to college, she was shocked to find out that not everyone kept turkey vultures and owls in the backyard. Over the years, she has kept more than 170 wild animals in a home in New York State. Most of them migrate in autumn; however, while they stay with George, they often become characters in her books and stories.

To research an article for *Reader's Digest*, George traveled to Alaska to observe scientists who were working on wolf communication. At one point, one of the men walked into a wolf's pen and gently bit the wolf on the top of its nose. The wolf sat down in front of the man, and the two of them communicated in soft whimpers. That incident stayed with George. Although she never wrote the article that she had been researching, she took what she had learned about Alaskan wolves and humans and turned it into a novel, which went through three extensive drafts. In fact, even the title changed numerous times. What began as "The Voice of the Wolf" became "Wolf! Wolf?," "Wolf Girl," "The Cry of the Wolf," and "Wolf Song" before finally being titled *Julie of the Wolves*.

In the book, a thirteen-year-old Inuit girl, Julie, runs away from an arranged marriage and survives on the Alaskan tundra. Nurtured by a wolf pack for many months, Julie learns to communicate with them — and to appreciate their unique society. She bravely encounters conflict after conflict, but in a bittersweet conclusion, she faces the fact that "the hour of the wolf and the Eskimo is over."

Readers not only learn about the tensions between the Inuit and white cultures, they learn about the magnificent wolves who roam the same land. With this awareness, readers of all ages grow to appreciate that as fellow creatures humans and wolves share the same earth. This theme, fascinating scientific information, and a determined and endearing protagonist have made this Newbery Medal winner extremely popular with teachers and children for over thirty years.

The Wind in the Willows

Written by Kenneth Grahame (1859–1932)
Illustrated by Ernest H. Shepard (1879–1976)
Published in 1908 by Charles Scribner's Sons
Ages 8 to 11   259 pages

Children's book writers often pursue a variety of professions before they decide to create something for children. Without question, *The Wind in the Willows* stands as the best children's book ever written by a banker. In fact, Kenneth Grahame distinguished himself as one of the youngest secretaries in the history of the Bank of England.

But his late-in-life marriage set him on the path to another destiny. At forty-one, Grahame became a father. When his only son, Alastair, nicknamed Mouse, turned four, Grahame began to tell him nightly bedtime stories — about moles, water rats, and a character named Toad. If father and son were separated from each other, Grahame continued the sagas by mail. Eventually, Elspeth Grahame convinced her husband to expand these letters into a book.

In a few idealized acres of English countryside, Mole, Rat, Badger, and the irrepressible Toad of Toad Hall get involved in one scheme after another. Toad carries the plot and adventure forward — discovering the joy of motoring, stealing a car, going to prison, escaping by dressing up as a woman, hijacking a train, and ransacking a barge. Yet each character basically longs to return home. Rat's river home, in particular, holds appeal for all those who enjoy "messing about in boats." Along with these unforgettable characters and their exploits, *The Wind in the Willows* contains some of the most lyrical passages in a children's book, including "The Piper at the Gates of Dawn," one of the few truly spiritual pieces of writing in the canon.

Grahame found a less-than-committed publisher — one who refused to offer him any advance money. At various times entitled "Mr. Mole and His Mates," "The Mole and the Water Rat," and "The Wind in the Reeds," *The Wind in the Willows* appeared in England in October 1908 and was published that same year in the United States because of the recommendation and sponsorship of President Theodore Roosevelt. Early reviews of the book varied in their enthusiasm, and the book had a very slow beginning.

In an attempt to increase interest in *The Wind in the Willows*, and because the original book had not been illustrated, Kenneth Grahame asked the great English illustrator Arthur Rackham to create some artwork for the story. But Rackham had too many commissions at the time. However, in the 1930s *The Wind in the Willows* grew in popularity with the appearance of A. A. Milne's stage version, *Toad of Toad Hall*. One of the book's greatest advocates,

Milne called it a "Household Book. By a Household Book, I mean a book which everyone in the household loves and quotes continually ever afterwards. . . . But it is a book that makes you feel that, though everybody in the house loves it, it is only you who really appreciates it at its true value."

Around the time of the play, Ernest Shepard, the illustrator of Milne's *Winnie-the-Pooh,* brought Grahame's characters to life with drawings that have been enjoyed by readers for seven decades. While he worked on the illustrations for the book, he went to meet with Kenneth Grahame, at that time in his seventies. Grahame said to Shepard, "I love these little people, be kind to them." Readers have echoed his sentiments through the years — and have taken these little people into their homes and their hearts.

The People Could Fly:
American Black Folktales

Written by Virginia Hamilton (1936–2002)
Illustrated by Leo and Diane Dillon (both b. 1933)
Published in 1985 by Alfred A. Knopf
Ages 8 to 11   178 pages

One day Virginia Hamilton confided her disappointment about the rejection of her adult novel to her college friend Janet Schulman. Schulman remembered a story that Hamilton had written in college, about a Watutsi princess, and suggested that it would make an excellent children's novel. The resulting book, *Zeely,* launched Hamilton's career in 1967.

Many years later, Schulman, now a publisher, bemoaned the lack of anthologies of African American folktales for children. She knew Hamilton's fascination with these stories and approached her about creating such a volume. Someone who had long been a student of slave folklore, Hamilton immediately seized upon this idea and began gathering, and retelling in her own style, that folklore. Hamilton wanted "to evoke the feeling for language and exquisite sense of story" of the tellers who had fashioned "these wonderful tales out of the good and bad of their lives." Told first by slaves, passed down orally, and finally gathered in collections, the stories in *The People Could Fly* gave slaves comfort and strength through endlessly hard times.

In a large, oversize volume, two dozen stories, illustrated with forty black-and-white drawings by the Dillons, have been arranged according to themes: animals; the real, the extravagant, and the fanciful; the supernatural; and freedom. The brilliance of Hamilton's writing, the attractive artwork, and an affordable price all helped garner great press coverage and reviews when the book appeared, and it quickly went back for reprint.

Published at a time when African American books often failed to do well financially, *The People Could Fly* emerged as a successful example of multicultural publishing and encouraged other such publishing efforts. In the course of her work, Hamilton would win an incredible number of awards, including the Newbery Medal, the Laura Ingalls Wilder Award, the Hans Christian Andersen Award, and a MacArthur Fellowship. This book, the most accessible of all of Hamilton's work, serves as an excellent introduction to the most revered and honored African American writer of her generation.

Redwall
....

By Brian Jacques (b. 1939)
Published in 1987 by Philomel Books
Ages 8 to 11   333 pages

Growing up in the rough neighborhood around the docks of Liverpool, England, Brian Jacques attended an inner-city school that produced two other international stars, Paul McCartney and George Harrison. Not encouraged to stay there, Jacques set out at fifteen to find adventure as a merchant seaman and become a student of the "University of Life." Returning to Liverpool a few years later, he found employment as a railway fireman, a long-shoreman, a long-distance truck driver, a bus driver, a boxer, a police officer, a postmaster, and a stand-up comic. Then he began writing a story for the children at the Royal Wavertree School for the Blind; he used descriptive language to paint pictures with words so that the children could actually see the scenes in their imaginations.

The residents of handsome Redwall Abbey, a place of serenity and peace, suddenly find their tranquillity interrupted by Cluny the Scourge, an insane rat with a horde of villainous followers. Matthias, a novice at the abbey, inspired by the legendary hero Martin, mobilizes the defense of Redwall. A cast of distinctive characters — Constance the Badger, Basil Stag Hare, Warbeak the Sparrow, and the abbot, Mortimer — all join forces to defeat Cluny and his gang. *Redwall* provides readers with all of the elements of great adventure fiction: derring-do, truly evil villains, and a clear sense of right and wrong. It also contains standard fantasy conventions: an awkward hero who discovers his true heritage, and the war between good and evil. But in *Redwall*, rats serve as villains and mice as heroes.

When *Redwall* appeared on the desk of the editor Patricia Lee Gauch, she knew the book would be a risky venture — it was much longer than the average novel for middle readers, contained warfare and violence, and included sections of difficult dialect. But she became its first American convert; then the library review media and librarians themselves, working with children, became its first advocates.

As each book in the Redwall series has been released, Brian Jacques has traveled extensively in the United States. He can imitate characters, set scenes, and help the audience paint word pictures in their minds. In fact, he personally conveys the enthusiasm that now millions of readers have found for the adventures of these peace-loving mice of Redwall Abbey.

The Phantom Tollbooth

Written by Norton Juster (b. 1929)
Illustrated by Jules Feiffer (b. 1929)
Published in 1961 by Epstein & Carroll
Ages 8 to 11   257 pages

An architect who wrote for relaxation from arduous planning projects, Norton Juster had received a grant from the Ford Foundation to create a book for children about how people experience cities. In 1959, to avoid writing this book, he began working on a short story — one that took on a life of its own. Juster viewed *The Phantom Tollbooth* as a way to procrastinate from his real responsibilities. He wrote without an outline and in no particular sequence, although he revised the book again and again to achieve the right pacing and word choice.

Juster and Jules Feiffer, the cartoonist, had been friends since the mid-1950s, when they lived in the same apartment building in Brooklyn Heights, New York. Although not intending to illustrate a children's book, Feiffer started to read what Juster had written and made drawings. As they worked together, Juster took great delight in describing things Feiffer might have difficulty drawing. The project continued with this lighthearted banter, and Feiffer modeled the Whether Man, on page 18, after Juster.

The Phantom Tollbooth shows the awakening of a lazy mind. The hero, Milo, finds himself bored with everything. Then one day he finds a package containing a tollbooth and an electric car, and he is transported to the Kingdom of Wisdom. In that land, with its tension between words and numbers, Milo is persuaded to bring the king's sisters, Rhyme and Reason, back to the kingdom. In his quest, he travels with the giant insect Humbug and the watchdog Tock, whose body contains a large alarm clock.

With a plot that twists and turns, the book excels in wordplay and the depiction of fantastic characters. Even the names of the minor characters entrance the reader: Duke of Definition, Minister of Meaning, Earl of Essence, Count of Connotation, and Undersecretary of Understanding. Often compared to Lewis Carroll's *Alice's Adventures in Wonderland,* the book might best be described as an exercise in thinking and writing outside the box.

Many reviewers believed the book too dependent on adult humor and far too sophisticated for children. However, even though college students and adults still love to quote from it, *The Phantom Tollbooth* has remained a staple of childhood reading for over forty years — as well as a testament to creative procrastination.

From the Mixed-up Files of
Mrs. Basil E. Frankweiler

By E. L. Konigsburg (b. 1930)
Published in 1967 by Atheneum Publishers
Newbery Medal
Ages 8 to 11   162 pages

Several elements came together in E. L. Konigsburg's mind as she constructed the ingenious plot for *From the Mixed-up Files of Mrs. Basil E. Frankweiler.* In 1965, she read in the *New York Times* about the purchase of a statue by the Metropolitan Museum of Art — *The Lady with the Primroses,* possibly the work of Leonardo da Vinci. At this same time, Konigsburg was reading *A High Wind in Jamaica,* a novel that tells of children who are captured by pirates. Then she attempted to organize a family picnic at Yellowstone National Park. Without a picnic table, the family crouched on the ground, and her children began complaining — about ants, the melting icing on their cupcakes, and the heat. Where, Konigsburg wondered, could these privileged children ever run away to if they left home? Nothing less elegant than the Museum of Modern Art would do. So Konigsburg began working on a book, basing the characters on her son and daughter. She even tested out her writing on them, taking in their reactions.

In *From the Mixed-up Files of Mrs. Basil E. Frankweiler,* when Claudia Kincaid finds herself bored with her suburban life, she decides to run away. Selecting her destination carefully, she chooses the Metropolitan Museum of Art and brings her younger brother Jamie along because he can bankroll the expedition. With all the appeal of *Robinson Crusoe,* the book has been given a setting infinitely more sumptuous than any desert island; at the Met, the siblings can wash in the museum fountain and sleep in antique canopy beds. During their stay, the children discover the secret of a new museum acquisition and meet the eccentric Mrs. Basil E. Frankweiler.

In 1968, Konigsburg's first novel, *Jennifer, Hecate, Macbeth, William McKinley, and Me, Elizabeth* won a Newbery Honor, and *From the Mixed-up Files,* her second novel, won the Newbery Medal. These awards brought both fame and professional recognition for the writer. However, it didn't seem to alter her relationship with her children. When a teacher asked Konigsburg's daughter what it was like having a famous writer as a mother, the girl responded: "Famous? My mother's just a mother. Why, I'd never argue with anyone famous, but I argue with my mother every day!"

Rabbit Hill

By Robert Lawson (1892–1957)
Published in 1944 by Viking Press
Newbery Medal
Ages 8 to 11   128 pages

Often a book gets written because a child demands to know what happens next. But in the case of *Rabbit Hill,* the motivating person proved to be Robert Lawson's insistent wife, Marie, who had fallen in love with the character of Little Georgie, a rabbit. Lawson had to keep writing at a rapid pace, he once said, to keep the family peace.

Robert and Marie Lawson had purchased property in Westport, Connecticut, which they named Rabbit Hill. Lawson's editor, May Massee, kept asking him to write a rabbit story from Rabbit Hill.

But the days turned into years before anything happened. Lawson always maintained that he never really wrote this book at all. "I pushed the pencil and pecked at the typewriter, but someone else certainly must have written it . . . I hadn't the faintest idea of what it was going to be or how it was to come out. . . . It just went ahead and wrote itself."

The novel that wrote itself seems even more timely today than it did in 1944. A new family moves into Rabbit Hill, and all the animals in the area are both excited about their arrival and worried about the consequences. But Lawson's gentle story supports the philosophy that all creatures, great and small, must find a way to inhabit this world together. As the final chapter states, "There Is Enough for All."

One morning after completing the book, Lawson saw a rabbit, who hopped along with him to the mailbox. In the mail that day came a letter from his editor, accepting the book. Sometime later, after Lawson had been ill, he headed to his studio, only to see another rabbit, sitting on the lawn, staring at the studio window. His wife maintained that there couldn't be any more good news about the book, enough had happened already. But the next day Lawson received a letter congratulating him on the Newbery Medal. Having won the Caldecott Medal four years earlier, Lawson became, in 1945, the only creator of children's books to win both awards.

A Wrinkle in Time

....

By Madeleine L'Engle (b. 1918)
Published in 1962 by Farrar, Straus and Giroux
Newbery Medal
Ages 8 to 11   211 pages

Because *A Wrinkle in Time* belonged to an elusive genre (both science fiction and fantasy) and because many thought it would be too difficult for young readers, twenty-six publishers rejected the book over a two-year period. Having finally advised the agent to withdraw the book, Madeleine L'Engle hosted a tea party for her visiting mother and some friends. One of those friends knew John Farrar of Farrar, Straus and Giroux, and eventually he accepted L'Engle's manuscript. But the publishing firm released only a small first edition, believing that the book would have limited appeal.

A science-fiction story, coming-of-age story, and philosophical novel, the book pulls together these complex strands into a compelling plot. Awkward and intense, Meg Murry and her precocious little brother, Charles Wallace, join forces with three beings — Mrs. Whatsit, Mrs. Who, and Mrs. Which. They all try to save Meg's physicist father from IT, a giant pulsing brain, the embodiment of evil. Ultimately, what saves the Murry family and Charles Wallace turns out to be Meg's ability to love rather than to hate.

A Wrinkle in Time has been called by critics "a good bad book." It even begins with the line considered to be one of the most clichéd in the English language, "It was a dark and stormy night." The original manuscript contains even more flaws and questionable material than did the finished book; reading sections, one can well understand why publishers rejected it. For many years, the book has appeared on the American Library Association's 100 Most Frequently Challenged Books list. Censors have decried the didactic qualities of the text or the overt Christianity; others have objected to Mrs. Which and her resemblance to a witch.

The strength of *A Wrinkle in Time* lies in the general sweep or scope of the novel, which gives young readers room for discussion. After the book won the Newbery Medal, it began reaching its audience in record numbers. By combining unconventional elements, Madeleine L'Engle created an engaging, action-packed story that has captured the imaginations of millions of children.

The Lion, the Witch, and the Wardrobe

Written by C. S. Lewis (1898–1963)
Illustrated by Pauline Baynes (b. 1922)

Published in 1950 by Macmillan
Ages 8 to 11   189 pages

When he was sixteen, C. S. Lewis saw a vivid image of a faun carrying an umbrella in a snowy wood. In 1939, he tried creating a book from this image and failed. Then nine years later, a lion leapt into a story, and Lewis began working on a book entitled "The Lion."

At this point in his life, Lewis, intensely unhappy and physically depleted, turned to the realm of his childhood reading, images, and thinking. Although he originally conceived the book to stand alone, he got swept up in the characters and the concepts and produced five books in the Narnia series in two years. In March 1949, he read the first story, "Lion," to his old friend Roger Lancelyn Green at dinner. Green helped him revise the manuscript, and shortly thereafter the book was accepted for publication.

In *The Lion, the Witch, and the Wardrobe,* four children have been evacuated during the London Blitz to stay with an elderly professor. They find a wardrobe leading to another world, Narnia. There, because of the spell of the evil White Witch, it is "always winter and never Christmas." The true ruler of Narnia, Aslan the Lion, has come to free the world from the spell of the White Witch. Eventually, Aslan dies for the sins of the children and rises again from the dead.

An Oxford scholar and teacher, Lewis met with a group called the Inklings, who shared work in progress. One of the Inklings, J.R.R. Tolkien, could not endure the Narnia stories, which he considered badly put together and flawed by a less-than-cohesive world structure. But Tolkien held exacting standards for his own fantasy and that of others.

From the beginning, children enjoyed the talking animals, fauns, and giants of this invented world. In *The Lion, the Witch, and the Wardrobe,* Lewis presents Christianity and Christian concepts to young readers. The Lion, Aslan, served as his allegory for Christ. However, he told the story so well that many children read the Narnia books and have no sense of its underpinnings. The books have endured not because of their philosophy, but because they

bring to life a magical world that readers want to enter again and
again.

Pippi Longstocking
....

Written by Astrid Lindgren (1907–2002)
Translated by Florence Lamborn (b. 1918)
Illustrated by Louis S. Glanzman (b. 1922)
Published in 1950 by Viking Press
Ages 8 to 11   160 pages

In 1941 the Swedish writer Astrid Lindgren's seven-year-old
daughter, sick in bed with pneumonia, asked her mother to tell
her a story about "Pippi Longstocking." Lindgren savored the
strange name, and, as she made up tales about Pippi, an unusual
but wonderful story emerged. On her daughter's tenth birthday,
Lindgren presented her with a completed manuscript of the book.
Although she'd been telling Pippi stories for three years, they were
actually written down only after Lindgren sprained her ankle and
found herself laid up in bed for several weeks. She later believed
that Pippi "was just waiting for someone to pick her up and write
about her."

Pippilotta Delicatessa Windowshade Mackrelmint Ephraim's
Daughter Longstocking, Pippi for short, lives without parents in
the middle of a town. Amazingly strong, she can pick up her own
horse, and she operates with great independence. Pippi dictates
the principles of her own upbringing; she nags herself about going
to bed at night, an amusing reversal of the usual role of the child.
An outrageous heroine, Pippi continually invents ways to entertain
herself and her more traditional friends, Tommy and Annika.

A revision of Lindgren's manuscript won a writing competition sponsored by a Swedish publishing house in 1945. But when
Lindgren submitted the final book for publication, she added this
tongue-in-cheek plea: "In the hope that you won't notify the Child
Welfare Committee." Possibly she knew that a character so origi-

nal and breaking so many of society's rules was bound to be controversial. Although some positive reviews appeared, one famous attack read, "Pippi is something unpleasant that scratches the soul." The badly behaved, impertinent heroine received condemnation from many different sources, sometimes being called "totally antisocial rubbish." And the criticism became even more pronounced in Sweden when *Pippi Longstocking* was read on the radio.

Now with the controversy long gone, a theme park, Astrid Lindgren's World in Vimmerby, Sweden, celebrates the book and characters. The winner of the Hans Christian Andersen Award for the body of her work, Lindgren was consistently mentioned in her lifetime as a contender for the Nobel Prize for Literature. In her attempt to comfort a sick child, she envisioned the perfect fantasy heroine — one who lives without supervision but with endless money to execute her schemes.

In the Year of the Boar and Jackie Robinson

Written by Bette Bao Lord (b. 1938)
Illustrated by Marc Simont (b. 1915)
Published in 1984 by Harper & Row
Ages 8 to 11   169 pages

Most classic books for the young result from years of dedication to the craft of writing for children. On occasion, a gem gets written by someone who has devoted a lifetime to other things — like the adult writer Bette Bao Lord.

Chinese-born Bette Bao, the daughter of a diplomat, came to the United States in 1946. When the Communists took over in 1949, the Baos settled here permanently. They kept their Chinese customs and ways, even though Bao Lord received her education in American schools. She worked from the age of twelve to help finance her own education, first learning to be a typist. After stints as a dancer and as a diplomat, Bao Lord wrote *Eighth Moon* to tell the story of her sister Sansan, who had been left behind in China and had grown up during the Communist regime. While Bao Lord's husband, the diplomat Winston Lord, traveled with Henry Kissinger, she eventually accompanied him to see the land of her childhood.

After struggling with a magazine article about being a Chinese girl growing up in Brooklyn, Bao Lord decided to shift the perspective and write the story from a child's point of view. At the age of eight, Bao Lord attended P.S. 8 in Brooklyn. As she worked to master English, she found that after she embraced the Brooklyn Dodgers, her fellow students accepted her.

In a heavily autobiographical novel that covers one year, 1947, Shirley Temple Wong makes the transition from the pampered child of an affluent, traditional Chinese family to an American youngster, coping with an entirely different culture. Shirley struggles with English, takes on baseball with passion, and becomes an ardent fan of the Brooklyn Dodgers. As Shirley triumphs, she proves that America truly can be the land of opportunities for immigrants.

With expressive drawings by the Caldecott Medal winner Marc Simont, the book captures the American love of sports and how that passion brings about community. It also provides one of our best written accounts of the assimilation of a foreign-born child into American culture.

The New Way Things Work

By David Macaulay (b. 1946)
Published in 1998 by Walter Lorraine/Houghton Mifflin
Ages 8 to 11   400 pages

Born in England in the Manchester steel area, David Macaulay grew up in a household where everyone created things. His father, a textile engineer, loved to fashion toys and wood carvings.

In the evenings, the family sat around in the kitchen, its coal stove the only source of heat, and made things — sewing, knitting, woodworking. "By the time we got out of that kitchen, we actually believed that creativity and craftsmanship were desirable — even normal." As a young boy, David Macaulay had already become fascinated with the way things work.

When Macaulay came to America as an eleven-year-old, he spoke with a funny accent, but he drew, very well, to impress those around him. Trained at the Rhode Island School of Design as an architecture student, he thought that architecture would be an artistic but still safe professional choice. However, he went on to teach art in a junior high school and returned to RISD to work with illustration students.

In the early 1970s, Macaulay wrote what he believed to be an innovative picture book, *Etienne and the Gargoyles of Gastonne* — a story about a French gargoyle beauty pageant. Although the initial concept now seems quite ridiculous, Macaulay traveled to the Houghton Mifflin offices in Boston to see the editor Walter Lorraine and talk about the book. "That's a magnificent drawing of the gargoyles against Notre Dame," said Lorraine. "Are you interested in cathedrals? Why not tell the story of the building instead?" And, of course, David Macaulay realized that he had a great deal to say about that topic. He returned home, coming back in a few months with the dummy of a book. It garnered him a $1000 advance against royalties, and he took the money to go to Amiens, north of Paris. He then sketched for three months, an extremely short period of time for such an ambitious undertaking, *Cathedral: The Story of Its Construction*.

But compared to Macaulay's most ambitious undertaking, *The Way Things Work,* his first book looks like a cakewalk. Macaulay has always put an incredible amount of effort into each project. His books take at least a year or more to develop, and if the deadlines don't allow for the breathing space, then he makes the time he needs by not sleeping. Often while working on a book, he shuts himself up in a room, sometimes not coming out for days.

For *The Way Things Work,* an enormous project, which actually features a woolly mammoth as a protagonist, Macaulay demonstrated in detailed drawings how hundreds of objects work: holograms, helicopters, airplanes, bits and bytes, locks, can openers, levers. For anyone, adult or child, with a practical mind, the book provides hours, if not years, of enjoyable reading. And ten years after its publication, Macaulay published a revised volume, *The New Way Things Work,* which moved the book into the computer and technical age.

A *New York Times* bestseller when it first appeared and a winner of the Boston Globe–Horn Book Award for information books, *The Way Things Work* takes technical expertise and mixes it with more than a dollop of humor. *The New Way Things Work* shows how the greatest information books for children can stand on their own merits in adult reference collections. In this book and others, David Macaulay proves himself the consummate teacher — showing how both learning and teaching can be totally enjoyable.

Winnie-the-Pooh

....

Written by A. A. Milne (1882–1956)
Illustrated by Ernest H. Shepard (1879–1976)
Published in 1926 by E. P. Dutton
Ages 8 to 11   161 pages

At the Donnell Library Center at the New York Public Library, some old — and very valuable — toys live permanently. They once belonged to Christopher Robin Milne, an English boy, who received a small stuffed bear on his first birthday. That bear, first named Edward Bear, later Winnie-the-Pooh, acquired several friends — Piglet, Eeyore, Owl, Rabbit, Kanga, Roo, and Tigger. Now preserved for the delight of other children, these toys generated one of the best-loved books of all time.

Like children everywhere, Christopher made up stories about these animals; his mother joined in, giving each character a distinct voice. Because of her encouragement, Alan Milne, a poet and playwright, began to write an occasional poem and story about the bear, Pooh, and Christopher's other toys. He not only recorded

Christopher's fantasies, he added his own wonderful blend of whimsy and imagination.

In the magical Hundred Acre Wood, the animals and Christopher Robin have memorable adventures — whether they are building a trap for a Heffalump, planning an "exposition" to the North Pole, or trying to kidnap baby Roo. The first sentence remains one of the most memorable in the English language: "Here is Edward Bear, coming downstairs now, bump, bump, bump, on the back of his head, behind Christopher Robin."

One Saturday morning, Ernest Shepard, without an appointment, called on Milne at his home with a portfolio of sketches. Although surprised to see an uninvited guest, Milne looked at Shepard's portfolio and loved the drawings. Shepard went on to illustrate Milne's book of poems, *When We Were Very Young;* later Shepard created the now classic drawings for *Winnie-the-Pooh.*

Sadly, Christopher Milne suffered emotional anguish because of this delightful book. As he grew older, he found himself mercilessly teased about his childhood and hated being perceived as a storybook character. Although his father knew how to craft brilliant fiction, he forgot to change the names to protect the innocent.

Today the toys at the Donnell Library look old and battered. But for each new reader, the vitality of Pooh and his friends comes alive every time the book is opened. Not only does *Winnie-the-Pooh* stand as one of the great toy stories of all time — it is simply one of the greatest books of all time.

Anne of Green Gables

By Lucy Maud Montgomery (1874–1942)
Published in 1908 by L. C. Page
Ages 8 to 11   308 pages

Writing served as an emotional release for L. M. Montgomery. She was raised in the small Prince Edward Island town of Cavendish by dour Scots Presbyterian grandparents. They were not really equipped to handle her, and as a young girl she channeled her emotion into creating stories. She lived most vividly in the book worlds of the romantic writers — Scott, Tennyson, Austen, and the Brontë sisters — who influenced her own work. Knowing she wanted to be a writer, she created hundreds of stories and achieved immediate success with her first published novel.

Around 1895 she jotted a story idea in one of her notebooks: an elderly couple apply to an orphan asylum for a boy, but by mistake a girl is sent. Montgomery first intended the story to be a mere seven chapters long, ideal for a serial treatment in a Sunday school paper. But the redheaded, determined, engaging Anne Shirley took on a life of her own. Montgomery became the first of a long list of people to fall in love with Anne. But the writer had trouble finding a publishing firm that felt the same way. After several rejections, she finally sent the manuscript to a small Boston firm, L. C. Page and Company.

Although the Page brothers intended to reject the manuscript too, a young girl on the staff from Prince Edward Island fought for it. They agreed to publish it but had little faith in the project, offering Montgomery either an outright fee of $500 or a royalty of 9 cents a book. Fortunately, she accepted the royalty. Published in June 1908, *Anne of Green Gables* became an immediate bestseller, with six printings in six months, selling more than 19,000 copies. Montgomery's first royalty check came to $1730. Positive reviews greeted this new arrival, and Montgomery particularly cherished a letter from Mark Twain, who found Anne the most lovable child in fiction since Lewis Carroll's Alice.

The minute Anne Shirley arrives at the farmhouse called Green Gables, she knows that she wants to stay forever. But she fears the Cuthberts will send her back to the orphanage, as she is not quite what they expected. Anne proves to be not what anyone expects, but all eventually succumb to her charm — her enormous imagination and great vitality.

Montgomery continued Anne's saga in seven subsequent volumes. Eventually, the young heroine became inextricably entwined in readers' minds with the locale of the novels, Prince Edward Island in southeastern Canada. The books about Anne have made this haven a destination for many travelers. Visitors can see, among other things, the house that inspired Green Gables, run by the Canadian Park Service, and the L. M. Montgomery Museum, which displays Montgomery's wedding dress.

Movies, television, and theater productions over the years have also tried to capture the charm of Anne Shirley. Anne, who called her special friends "kindred spirits," has found legions of them, all over the world.

The Great Fire

By Jim Murphy (b. 1947)
Published in 1995 by Scholastic
Newbery Honor Book
Ages 8 to 11   144 pages

Jim Murphy found history boring as a child, merely a string of facts. Because he had an eye condition that went undetected, he had trouble as a student in grammar school. Consequently, he didn't even read a book until he was ten, and then he tackled *Moby-Dick*. For a period of time, Murphy worked in publishing, often observing the creation of information books for children — books such as Russell Freedman's *Lincoln: A Photobiography*. Then, rather than work on other people's books, he set out to write books himself — the kind of books that he would have liked to have encountered as a child.

For *The Great Fire*, Murphy drew upon a childhood incident. Exploring the woods with a group of boys, he and they inadvertently set a fire that got out of control. They all worked diligently to put it out, but the fire almost surrounded them. The memory of the smoke, the group working together to control the flames, and the fear of what might have happened stayed with Murphy all his life.

While working on another book, Murphy discovered the letter of Claire Innis, a twelve-year-old girl who survived the Chicago fire of 1871. He then searched for other eyewitness accounts: "I wanted readers to experience what it was like to see the fire approaching, hear its terrible roar, and feel the intense heat. So I began search-ing for other people who had barely escaped the consuming fire and left a written account of it."

One of the best photo-essay books for children ever published, *The Great Fire* sweeps readers up in the emotion and the events of this catastrophe; the narrative pulses along, much like the fire it-self. Having taken on increased resonance since September 11, *The Great Fire* shows how, after enormous devastation, a city can re-build itself, creating something finer than what already existed. Al-though classified, justifiably, as nonfiction, the book — with the benefit of Murphy's superb storytelling skill — reads like a dra-matic novel, urging readers to turn the pages to learn what actually happened in the great Chicago fire.

Rascal

Written by Sterling North (1906–1974)
Illustrated by John Schoenherr (b. 1935)
Published in 1963 by E. P. Dutton
Newbery Honor Book
Ages 8 to 11   189 pages

Set in World War I, in rural Wisconsin, *Rascal* recounts the story of young Sterling North, a motherless boy whose father was often absent. Relying on his pets for company, Sterling sur-rounds himself with an impressive group — Wowser the Saint Bernard, various cats, a family of four skunks, and Poe, a pet crow. Then one day he finds a baby raccoon in the forest.

In a narrative that moves by months from May to April of the next year, Rascal learns to ride on the front of Sterling North's bike and shares his meals, fishing expeditions, and bed at night. In a totally satisfying but poignant ending, Rascal, having grown too large to be a pet, finds a life of his own: "He hesitated for a full min-ute, turned once to look back at me, then took the plunge and swam to the near shore. He had chosen to join that entrancing female somewhere in the shadows. I caught only one glimpse of them in a moonlit glade before they disappeared to begin their new life together."

Often in his lifetime, North received questions about the fate of his pet Rascal. Although he never saw Rascal again, he did keep his boyhood promise, made at the age of twelve, never again to shoot or trap any bird or animal.

Set in a time of enduring values, often viewed with nostalgia today, *Rascal* recounts an era when children like Sterling North found amusement with the wildlife and animals of the farmyard. In an attempt to preserve some of that past for posterity, in 1992 the Sterling North Society purchased North's childhood home in Edgerton, Wisconsin, where he lived with Rascal, and created a museum.

A history, family saga, and animal book, *Rascal* has sold more than 2.5 million copies in paperback and hardcover and been translated into at least eighteen languages. Sterling North also had a distinguished career as an essayist, critic, and series editor of North Star history books for Houghton Mifflin. But his most lasting contribution to the world of children's books remains this boyhood memoir — the biography of a beloved pet.

Mrs. Frisby and the Rats of NIMH

Written by Robert C. O'Brien (1918–1973)
Illustrated by Zena Bernstein
Published in 1971 by Atheneum Publishers
Newbery Medal
Ages 8 to 11   233 pages

In a media-crazed age, Robert C. O'Brien's path to fame seems refreshing. Because he worked at *National Geographic* and because the esteemed magazine frowned on outside writing by staff members, Robert Leslie Conly adopted a pseudonym based on his mother's maiden name and published his children's novels covertly. However, when he won the Newbery Medal for *Mrs. Frisby and the Rats of NIMH,* a public speech was required. But anyone inventive enough to create the plot of this novel could obviously find a solution for the dilemma. Conly simply asked his editor at Atheneum, Jean Karl, to read the talk he had prepared. Only at his death did it become known that the mild-mannered staff writer and the acclaimed novelist were one and the same person.

In a novel that combines talking animals with futuristic scientific speculation, Robert O'Brien quickly draws the reader into the problems of a family of field mice. A determined widow, Mrs. Frisby attempts to find a way to move her sick son before spring planting destroys them all. As a last resort, she consults the rats who live under the rosebush and finds an amazingly sophisticated society. These rats had once been part of an experimental group at the National Institute of Mental Health (NIMH), receiving a series of mind-enhancing drugs that also prolonged life. As the leader Nicodemus tells her, "By teaching us how to read, they taught us how to get away." Now, five years after their escape from NIMH, the group has been working on the Plan, a long-range vision of survival that doesn't involve stealing from others. The rats yearn to be self-supporting through their own efforts.

In a similar vein of independence, the author of *Mrs. Frisby and the Rats of NIMH* achieved his own notoriety only by the effort he put into writing the novel. Without book tours, media interviews, meeting and greeting people, talking to children, or any other kind of public appearance, Robert C. O'Brien gained his devoted following solely by writing one of the great science-fiction stories of the modern age.

Island of the Blue Dolphins

Written by Scott O'Dell (1898–1989)
Published in 1960 by Houghton Mifflin
Newbery Medal
Ages 8 to 11   184 pages

Scott O'Dell had known about the Lost Woman of San Nicolas Island, who had lived there, alone, from 1835 to 1853, for decades before he finally sat down to write about her. In a career that had taken him to Rome to film *Ben-Hur,* he was working as the book review editor for the *Los Angeles Times* when he finished *Island of the Blue Dolphins.* Because he did not really know who the audience would be, he gave the manuscript to Houghton Mifflin's West Coast sales representative. The children's department decided that, in fact, the book would be ideal for young readers. So at sixty-two, O'Dell became a children's book writer, by chance, and won the prestigious Newbery Medal for his efforts. He continued to write children's books until his death at ninety-one.

For his first-person survival story, O'Dell wanted a simple language pattern and chose iambic pentameter. Because so little of his protagonists' history was known, he could indulge in his talent for spinning tales. As Karana fights wild dogs, deals with the death of her brother, finds a dog companion, protects her food supplies, and tries to escape from the island, she faces her challenges with courage — and is transformed in the process.

Scott O'Dell believed that *Island of the Blue Dolphins* described how we have a "chance to come into a new relationship to other things around us. . . . Karana changed from a world where everything lived to be exploited to a new and more meaningful order." That perspective, at the heart of the novel, makes it even more timely for today's reader than it was when it was published over forty years ago.

O'Dell had requested that after his death his ashes be scattered over the Pacific Ocean, the water that had always defined his life. After a celebratory ceremony, the skipper turned the boat around to return to the Mission Bay Harbor in San Diego. Suddenly, a dozen dolphins appeared, leaping in the water to escort the boat until it reached the channel entrance to its destination. For those present, a line in the book suddenly took on new meaning: "More than anything, it was the blue dolphins that took me back home."

Bridge to Terabithia

....

Written by Katherine Paterson (b. 1932)
Illustrated by Donna Diamond (b. 1950)
Published in 1977 by T. Y. Crowell
Newbery Medal
Ages 8 to 11   128 pages

After writing stories about feudal Japan, Katherine Paterson wanted to work on a contemporary American novel. Then shortly after she was diagnosed with cancer, lightning struck and killed her son's best friend. Paterson began thinking about death, love, the nature of healing. "How can I say that I want him to 'get over it' as though having loved and been loved were some sort of disease?" Because her editor, Virginia Buckley, suggested that Paterson write about this experience for young people, she located a kernel of a story but found that as she worked on it, she grew colder and colder with each page of writing, as if she were frozen. Eventually she confessed to a friend that she was having trouble writing about the girl's death. Her friend said, "I don't think it's [the child's] death you can't face. I think it's yours." With that insight, Paterson completed the final novel in a few weeks, writing in a kind of fever.

Bridge to Terabithia recounts the growing friendship between a country boy, Jesse, and an uprooted city girl, Leslie. As they get to know each other, they invent the magical kingdom of Terabithia. In the initial draft of the book, Terabithia emerged, fully realized in the formal language of high fantasy. Paterson rewrote these sections, filling in few details about the actual kingdom. But over the years children have supplied their own fantasies about Terabithia; in this way, readers participate with the author in writing the book.

A groundbreaking novel about the death of a child, the book received the Newbery Medal, in part because of Paterson's reputation, but also because of her obvious humanity in treating a difficult subject. Since that time every conceivable children's book award has been bestowed on Katherine Paterson, including the

BOOKS FOR MIDDLE READERS 🦋 119

Hans Christian Andersen Award, and she has traveled internationally as an emissary for American children's literature. Although she has written many outstanding books, including *Lyddie* and *The Great Gilly Hopkins, Bridge to Terabithia* remains her most popular. For as she herself has said: "The time a child needs a book about life's dark passages is before he or she has had to experience them. We need practice with loss, rehearsal for grieving, just as we need preparation for decision making."

Hatchet

Written by Gary Paulsen (b. 1939)
Published in 1987 by Bradbury Press
Newbery Honor Book
Ages 8 to 11   189 pages

A lifelong outdoorsman with a love of nature, Gary Paulsen wanted to create a book like *Hatchet* all his life. But the book was actually inspired by a visit to the Hershey, Pennsylvania, Middle School in April 1986. While talking to students about their passions, Paulsen realized that he should write the survival tale that had been brewing in his mind, and he dedicated the book to those children. In *Hatchet,* a troubled city boy, thirteen-year-old Brian Robeson, manages to survive for two months in the Canadian wilderness, with only a hatchet to aid him. Remarkable for its fast-paced action and harrowing escapes, the book evokes the sights, sounds, and feeling of the wilderness.

According to Paulsen, "I was concerned that everything that happened to Brian should be based on reality. . . . I did not want him to do things that wouldn't or couldn't really happen in his situation. Consequently, I decided to write only of things that had happened to me or things I purposely did to make certain they would work for Brian."

Paulsen, who had run the Iditarod, drew on his experiences surviving in nature. He himself had been attacked by a moose and by particularly virulent mosquitoes. But he decided to spare Brian the swarms of black flies, horseflies, and deerflies that he had also encountered. One of Paulsen's hardest tasks was to start a fire with a hatchet and a rock, but eventually he accomplished this feat in four hours. He then tried eating snapping turtle's eggs, which he describes as tasting like "old motor oil or tired Vaseline." Although he was not successful at getting them down, he decided that Brian, being much hungrier, would be able to do so.

Paulsen's editor, Barbara Lalicki, shared his love of survival stories. Lalicki postponed the publication of the book to allow for several more rewrites. Her attention to detail, combined with Paulsen's experiences, shaped a book that leaves readers feeling that they have been surviving alone in the wilderness.

Consequently, *Hatchet,* the best modern survival story for children, proves to be far more exciting and believable than anything they can see on television or in the movies.

Tom's Midnight Garden

Written by Philippa Pearce (b. 1920)
Illustrated by Susan Einzig (b. 1922)
Published in 1959 by J. B. Lippincott
Ages 8 to 11   229 pages

Having contracted tuberculosis, Philippa Pearce lay in a hospital bed in Cambridge, England, for most of the summer of 1951. She thought constantly of her parents' home, an old mill house and garden past which the river Cam flowed. Confined to the hospital, she traveled to that home in her imagination. Eventually, she went back to work but decided she wanted to write a children's book with this setting. Then the character of Tom Long began to form in her mind.

After going reluctantly to stay with relations while his brother has measles, Tom finds that at night, when the clock strikes thirteen, he can enter a magical garden. There he skates on the ice for miles and builds a tree house with an enchanting girl, Hatty, a lonely orphan. But although Tom stays the same age, Hatty begins to grow older. Increasingly involved in the life of the midnight garden, Tom ultimately comprehends that Hatty lives in the same place as he but a different time.

For this ghost story grounded in the real world, Pearce provided photographs and pictures of the specific settings for the illustrator. Consequently, many of the drawings reflect actual details from Pearce's family home. Besides its superb delineation of place, the book also artfully examines many ideas, such as the similarity of childhood and old age. Using a walled garden, because it represents the sheltered security of early childhood, Pearce explores time and the changes it brings about in people. As she once said: "I think I write out of present experience; but present experience includes — sometimes painfully — the past."

The British critic John Rowe Townsend considers *Tom's Midnight Garden* the greatest British novel written since World War II. Some books appeal mainly to children, while others speak to those who love children's books. Although *Tom's Midnight Garden* belongs in the latter category, it can still provide a wonderful reading experience for an entire family. For adults, it remains one of those rare children's books that can be read in every decade of life with a deeper understanding and appreciation.

The Westing Game

By Ellen Raskin (1928–1984)
Published in 1978 by E. P. Dutton
Newbery Medal
Ages 8 to 11   185 pages

In 1976, in the bicentennial year, Ellen Raskin began drafting a novel with a few distinct components: a historical background, a puzzle mystery, the forging of wills, the death of a millionaire, and imperfect heirs. With a working title of "Eight Imperfect Pairs of

Heirs," the book that slowly evolved surprised her. This seemingly simple story chronicles how the will of Samuel W. Westing, an eccentric millionaire, sends his heirs searching for his murderer. However, the simple plot grows amazingly complex with aliases, disguises, word games, and trickery.

Ellen Raskin came to writing through her work as an artist. A student of fine arts at the University of Wisconsin, she moved to New York to set up shop as a free-lance commercial artist. After designing about a thousand book jackets, she also began illustrating children's books with ingenious pictures created from words and letters. Finally, she shifted to straight prose. In fact, she had always hoped to win the Caldecott Medal for illustration. Instead, she won a Newbery Medal for *The Westing Game,* a book many thought simply too much fun to win the highest literary award.

In her Newbery speech, Ellen Raskin said, "I write and design my books to look accessible to the young reader . . . there will be no endless seas of gray type. I plan for margins wide enough for hands to hold, typographic variations for the eyes to rest, decorative breaks for the mind to breathe. I want my children's books to look like a wonderful place to be."

Little editorial correspondence exists between Raskin and her editor, Ann Durell, because they talked about the book over lunch or while Raskin cut her editor's hair. However, anyone who wants to see various drafts of the manuscript, and listen to Raskin speak about *The Westing Game,* can go to the following Web site: www .education.wisc.edu/ccbc/wisauth/raskin/intro.htm. The site provides an appreciation of the writing and rewriting that was required to produce this elegant and inventive mystery.

Harry Potter and the Sorcerer's Stone

By J. K. Rowling (b. 1965)
Illustrated by Mary GrandPré (b. 1954)
Published in 1998 by Arthur A. Levine/Scholastic
Ages 8 to 11   312 pages

On a train to London in 1990, J. K. Rowling looked out the window, and the character of Harry Potter sprang into her head. She felt that she could literally see him, including his round glasses and signature scar. With the train delayed for nearly four hours, she sat writing and developing characters — Nearly Headless Nick, Peeves the Poltergeist, Hermione, Ron, and Harry. After some time in Portugal, Rowling returned to England with some drafts of *Harry Potter*. She decided to finish the manuscript, although she had to borrow money from friends. Leaving her unheated flat, she would put her daughter in a stroller, push her about the streets until the child fell asleep, and then nurse a cup of coffee at her brother-in-law's restaurant while she wrote. She often went without food and endured depression.

Five years later, after she had completed the manuscript, she tried unsuccessfully to get it published and finally located an agent to represent her. Although nine English houses rejected *Harry Potter*, the agent sent it to a small British publisher, Bloomsbury, and Barry Cunningham took on the project. Although he loved the book, Cunningham advised Rowling to get a day job because children's books make so little money for their authors.

The American editor Arthur Levine read a copy of the book on the way home from the Bologna book fair, the international fair for the exchange of children's books. Swept up in the narrative, which exhibited the classic qualities of Roald Dahl's *James and the Giant Peach* and Philip Pullman's *The Golden Compass*, Levine secured the American rights for the book in an auction, paying over $100,000 — an extremely high and risky advance for an unknown author. Already, Harry Potter had begun his ascent to stardom.

As a way to entice children into reading, few stories surpass the Harry Potter novels. In *Harry Potter and the Sorcerer's Stone*, Harry, his new friends Hermione Granger and Ron Weasley, and other classmates enter Hogwarts School of Witchcraft and Wizardry. Although the book takes place in the 1990s, the story has an old-fashioned feeling; children get letters, delivered by owls, rather than exchanging e-mail. At school Harry finds that he possesses particular talent for the game of quidditch, which requires immense skill and combines flying, goalkeeping, and broomsticks. With the help of his friends and of Hagrid, a giant, and Albus Dumbledore, the headmaster, Harry unearths an old enemy who has camped out beneath the school — the evil Voldemort.

Rowling has gone on to transform Harry's world into a series, which contains a number of stock ingredients for successful children's books: a school story, an orphan story, a friendship chronicle, and the struggle between good and evil. Although she invented games like quidditch for her saga, Rowling tends to mine old, established forms, but develops them masterfully. The books also depend on class struggle — between those born to parents with magic blood and those born to Muggles, nonmagic parents. Like Oliver Twist and David Copperfield, Harry Potter experiences early tragedy in his life and lives with cruel surrogate parents. An apparently ordinary child, he turns out to be extraordinary.

No matter how much anyone loved the first book, no one anticipated the Harry Potter phenomena. Each volume has climbed to the top of the *New York Times* bestseller list; the fifth volume sold 5 million copies in the first few days of its release. (J. K. Rowling, once poverty-stricken, became wealthier than the queen of England.) Scores of young people, many who had remained oblivious to the charms of reading, found themselves beguiled by Harry; movies adapted from the books set box-office records.

Any book this popular will naturally find its detractors. Although the struggle between good and evil underscores most fantasies, some readers critical of the contents of these books took umbrage at Harry Potter, destroying copies in public and attempting to get the books banned from schools and libraries. For the last four years, the Harry Potter series has been among the most challenged books in America.

Nothing like Harry Potter — with J. K. Rowling and her rags-to-riches personal story, and with the characters so quickly becoming part of the American lexicon — has ever been seen in the book world. Like its protagonist, a seemingly ordinary book became extraordinary.

Holes

....

By Louis Sachar (b. 1954)
Published in 1998 by Frances Foster/Farrar, Straus and Giroux
Newbery Medal
Ages 8 to 11   233 pages

If *The Wind in the Willows* stands as the best book written by a banker, *Holes* distinguishes itself as the best book created by a lawyer. In Louis Sachar's case, however, he had already established himself as a writer of appealing, but very light and frothy, middle-grade novels, such as *Sideways Stories from Wayside School* and *There's a Boy in the Girls' Bathroom*. But with *Holes,* he surpassed everyone's expectations of his talents and abilities.

Hot Texas summers inspired Sachar to write the book. "Anyone who has ever tried to do yard work in Texas in July can easily imagine Hell to be a place where you are required to dig a hole five feet deep and five feet across day after day under the brutal Texas sun." As he wrote, Sachar envisioned the place first, Camp Green Lake, with no lake and hardly anything green, and then the characters and plot grew out of this setting. In the process, buried treasure, a famous outlaw named Kissin' Kate Barlow, and yellow-spotted lizards all emerged from Sachar's heat-infected brain. In *Holes,* the hero, Stanley Yelnats (whose name reads the same way forward or backward), finds himself unfairly incarcerated in a boot camp for juvenile delinquents. Here the inmates have to dig the enormous holes of Sachar's imagination as they are spurred on by a villainous warden with venom-tipped nails.

To weave all these elements together, Sachar wrote and rewrote the book five times before even giving it to his editor, Frances Foster. This diligence served him well, for *Holes* — a rare winner of the triple crown in children's literature (National Book Award, Boston Globe–Horn Book Award, and Newbery Medal) — captivated reviewers and critics for its inventiveness, structure, pacing, and child appeal. With a screenplay by Sachar, *Holes* was also transformed into a very entertaining movie.

If there is any moral or lesson in the book, Louis Sachar believes it to be a simple one: "Reading is fun." It would be difficult to find a fan of *Holes* who doesn't agree with him.

The Cricket in Times Square

Written by George Selden (1929–1989)
Illustrated by Garth Williams (1912–1996)
Published in 1960 by Farrar, Straus and Giroux
Newbery Honor Book
Ages 8 to 11   151 pages

George Selden Thompson, a Yale University graduate, came to New York to write plays. When a friend working for Viking Press suggested that he try his hand at a children's book, he invented *The Dog That Could Swim Under Water,* a rather feeble attempt. Selden took the advice given to him by Noel Coward at a party: "Press on!" Late one night, when he heard a cricket chirp in the Times Square subway station, a story idea formed instantly.

Selden, who grew up in rural Connecticut, drew on themes familiar to him: daily life in New York City, a love of music, especially opera, and the longing of an urban dweller for the country. In this inventive talking-animal fantasy, unlikely forces save a failing business. Several well-developed characters move the story along: Mario Bellini and his parents, who operate an unsuccessful newspaper stand in the Times Square subway; Chester, a liverwurst-loving cricket; Tucker, a good-natured scavenger mouse; and the warmhearted cat Harry. After Chester befriends Mario, he uses his operatic talents to bring customers to the newsstand. But still longing for the country, Chester leaves fame, fortune, and New York behind — to return home.

With a blend of satire and fancy in his artwork, Garth Williams proved to be an ideal illustrator for the book, just as he was for *Charlotte's Web.* Like Selden, Williams adeptly delineates character and emphasizes the humor in the text. The two men were paired for this book by Selden's publisher, and they developed a friendship that extended over many sequels.

The Cricket in Times Square is an ideal book to read aloud, although many readers prefer to avoid the exaggerated Chinese dialect of the character Sai Fong. The totally engaging story presents a vision of city life in which community and supportive relationships flourish. *Charlotte's Web* and *The Cricket in Times Square,* with their themes of loyalty and enduring friendship, often appeal to the same readers.

The Witch of Blackbird Pond

By Elizabeth George Speare (1908–1994)
Published in 1958 by Houghton Mifflin
Newbery Medal
Ages 8 to 11   223 pages

For her second children's novel, Elizabeth George Speare turned to her own town of Wethersfield, Connecticut, as a setting. One day, while walking by a stream with her husband, Speare imagined the presence of another figure, a solitary young woman. Choosing 1687, the year of the Connecticut Charter, she placed her story in a time when people believed in witches, and she drew actual testimony from local witchcraft trials. Even the character of Kit Tyler herself was based on a real emigrant from Barbados. Speare, who always liked to use orphans as characters because they had more control over their lives, found herself attracted to that girl.

An enchanting heroine with irrepressible flair, Kit Tyler arrives, unexpectedly, with seven trunks, at the home of her aunt and uncle in Wethersfield. An orphan from Barbados, Kit finds the chilly, gray New England difficult, as well as the suffocating Puritanism of her new surroundings. But she finds solace, freedom, and peace in the swampy meadows by Blackbird Pond, in the company of

Hannah Tupper, a kindred soul and Quaker. Eventually, the towns-people turn on Hannah, branding her as an infidel and witch, and Kit seeks to save her friend.

After spending a year and a half working on the novel, Speare sent it to Mary Silva Cosgrave, the editor who had rescued her first book, *Calico Captive,* from a pile of unsolicited manuscripts. Cosgrave found the manuscript for *The Witch of Blackbird Pond* to be the most perfectly crafted she had ever seen. Because Speare had been so thorough in her research and in the way she had pieced the book together, Cosgrave suggested only one minor correction before the book went to press.

The Newbery committee had similar feelings about the book's perfection. Although the details of the Newbery's selection process usually remain confidential, the chair of the committee revealed that *The Witch of Blackbird Pond* won the Newbery Medal unanimously on the first ballot, an extremely rare event. Since then, 4.5 million readers have taken to heart the story of Kit Tyler — one that explores Colonial history, independence of spirit, and the nature of prejudice.

Mary Poppins

....

Written by P. L. Travers (1899–1996)
Illustrated by Mary Shepard (1909–2000)
Published in 1934 by Reynal and Hitchcock
Ages 8 to 11   202 pages

Although many discover the book through the movie, the original Mary Poppins emerges as a good bit saltier and more mysterious than the woman portrayed by Julie Andrews. In fact, Mary Poppins appeared to be the alter ego for Pamela Lyndon Travers, who once remarked that *Mary Poppins* told the story of her own life. She said that "the idea of Mary Poppins has been blowing in and out of me, like a curtain at a window, all my life." Growing up in Australia, Travers had a series of nannies herself. One owned a parrot-headed umbrella.

In *Mary Poppins,* a vain, stern, proud, no-nonsense nanny arrives at Number 17 Cherry Tree Lane and takes charge of the Banks children, altering their lives forever. Mary Poppins can levitate the children to have tea on the ceiling. She can glue stars to the sky. Much like her predecessor in children's fiction, the engaging character Doctor Dolittle, Mary can speak to the animals and interpret animal speech for humans. But she always maintains that nothing extraordinary has happened.

Mary Shepard, who added lively and expressive artwork to the book, actually got the assignment only after her more famous father, Ernest Shepard, illustrator of *Winnie-the-Pooh* and *The Wind in the Willows,* told the publisher he didn't have time to take on the work.

In the seventies and early eighties, *Mary Poppins,* like many books of its era, came under attack for racism and stereotypes. In typical P. L. Travers fashion, she took this matter into her own hands and rewrote the sections others found offensive. Hence the chapter "Bad Tuesday" now contains the changes made in the 1981 revision.

However, even with minor alterations, Mary Poppins remains a unique character in the canon of children's literature — she stands squarely on the side of the children rather than authority. Opinionated and eccentric, Travers always maintained that "I don't write for children at all. I turn my back on them." But as an advocate for fun, entertainment, and a bit of anarchy, P. L. Travers created a character and a story that children enjoy and cherish. An ideal book to read aloud, it quickly convinces readers that the movie missed many of the best parts.

Charlotte's Web

....

Written by E. B. White (1899–1985)
Illustrated by Garth Williams (1912–1996)
Published in 1952 by Harper & Row
Newbery Honor Book
Ages 8 to 11   192 pages

Charlotte's Web features one of the best opening sentences in all of children's literature, "Where is Pa going with that ax?" From the beginning to the end of this book, the reader will enjoy the craft of a master storyteller. In *Charlotte's Web*, Fern, a young girl, and Charlotte, a spider, save the life of Wilbur, the runt pig of his litter. Charlotte accomplishes this miracle with language, five words in all, woven into her web: *some pig, terrific, radiant,* and *humble.* We catch a glimpse of Fern, as a young girl, in a brief moment in time. But the starring role belongs to a spider, a spider that E. B. White makes us care for and love.

White excels in character descriptions. "Charlotte is fierce, brutal, scheming, bloodthirsty — everything I don't like," Wilbur tells us. Templeton the rat "had no morals, no conscience, no scruples, no consideration, no decency, no milk of rodent kindness, no compunctions, no higher feelings, no friendliness, no anything." Although E. B. White notoriously disliked rats, in the end Templeton does more good than harm.

The lyrical language of the descriptive passages can take your breath away: "The barn was very large. It was very old. It smelled of hay and it smelled of manure. It smelled of the perspiration of tired horses and the wonderful sweet breath of patient cows. It often had a sort of peaceful smell — as though nothing bad could happen ever again in the world."

As White once wrote, "All that I ever hope to say is that I love the world." As a boy, E. B. White first found the world that he particularly cherished during summers in the Belgrade Lakes in Maine. His love of nature inspired all three of his children's books. The first of these, *Stuart Little,* took White about eighteen years to

write. *Charlotte's Web* emerged after a relatively short two-year ges-
tation process. It began as an essay for the *Atlantic Monthly* entitled
"Death of a Pig," which told how White tended an ailing pig, only
to have it die. The idea for the book came to White while he was
carrying a pail of slops to his pig and thinking about writing a children's book. He wanted a way to save a pig's life, and then he
started watching a large spider.

A seasoned *New Yorker* writer, Elwyn Brooks White was working
at the height of his craft in 1952 when he finished the book. His editor, Ursula Nordstrom, claimed that she never altered even a word
of the manuscript that was delivered to her and published that year.
She did, however, suggest that he change the title of the chapter
"The Death of Charlotte." In the final version, the chapter is titled
"The Last Day." Fifty thousand copies were printed immediately,
and *Charlotte's Web* went on to become the best-selling children's
paperback book in America.

But even masterpieces have their critics. Anne Carroll Moore,
the powerful head of Children's Services of the New York Public Library, wrote in *The Horn Book,* that she found White's book "hard
to take from so masterful a hand." Many believe that Moore played
a critical role in keeping the gold Newbery seal from adorning the
cover. Instead, Ann Nolan Clark's seldom-read *The Secret of the An-
des* triumphed over *Charlotte's Web* for the Newbery Medal.

Some of the early controversy surrounding the book no doubt
stemmed from White's unflinching honesty in presenting the issues of life and death. A story that faces death, loneliness, and loss,
Charlotte's Web also celebrates life and Wilbur's love of life. But it
renders a wide range of human and animal emotion. Most readers
find themselves crying when Charlotte dies, and White himself,
once making a commercial recording, choked as he read the words
"and no one was with her when she died."

Over fifty years after its publication, *Charlotte's Web* remains one
of the best-loved and most perfectly crafted children's books of all
times. Like its famous protagonist, Charlotte, the book is in a class
by itself.

Books for
Older Readers

Ages 11 to 12

The True Confessions
of Charlotte Doyle

By Avi (b. 1937)
Published in 1990 by Richard Jackson/Orchard Books
Newbery Honor Book
Ages 11 to 12   232 pages

If you imagine *Mutiny on the Bounty* with a female heroine, you have the basic plot of *The True Confessions of Charlotte Doyle*. In 1832, thirteen-year-old Charlotte sets out to sail from her boarding school in England to Providence, Rhode Island, to join her family. But hers proves to be an abnormal ocean crossing when she steps onto the ship of black-hearted Captain Jaggery. Given to view authority figures with the respect she would accord to her father, who owns the sailing line, Charlotte tells the captain of a planned mutiny. But then, after the cruel murder of two sailors, she realizes her error, dons a sailor suit, and joins the crew.

Avi first entered the realm of children's books as a character. His fourth-grade class was portrayed in Bette Bao Lord's book *In the Year of the Boar and Jackie Robinson,* and Avi made his debut as Irvie, the silent member of the group. A daydreamer in school, Avi had trouble as a student and suffered from dysgraphia, a writing dysfunction that manifests itself in bad spelling and word omissions.

However, when his son was born in 1970, he began writing for children and has always used only his childhood nickname as his nom de plume. Fortunately, he found an ideal editor in Richard Jackson, who himself has dyslexia. As Avi has said, "I have trouble writing, and he has trouble reading; that seems to be the core of our working relationship. . . . My hand holds the pencil. Dick sharpens it."

Avi had been working on another book, *The Man Who Was Poe,* when he began thinking about *The True Confessions of Charlotte*

Doyle. At first he thought he would write a mystery, entitled "The Seahawk," set on the high seas. But as he wrote, he cared more and more about Charlotte — and ultimately decided that it should become her book.

A strong, capable heroine, Charlotte stands on her own and wins over readers, just as she won over her creator. Avi brings readers along, breathless, as they watch the transformation of a very proper lady into a crew member of a pirate ship.

Tuck Everlasting

....

By Natalie Babbitt (b. 1932)
Published in 1975 by Farrar, Straus and Giroux
Ages 11 to 12   139 pages

In a thought-provoking book set in the late nineteenth century, ten-year-old Winnie Foster discovers a secret spring on her family's property; if she drinks the water, she will live forever. She also meets seventeen-year-old Jesse Tuck and his family; they haven't aged for eighty years. Around the property lurks the evil "man in the yellow suit," who intends to profit from the spring. Before the Tucks leave her, Jesse gives Winnie a bottle of the spring water, encouraging her to drink it when she turns seventeen — so that she will stay his age forever.

Before Natalie Babbitt set out to write *Tuck Everlasting,* she worked out a complete chronology and very clear ending. She did not even begin writing until she knew what was going to happen to the characters. The various drafts of the manuscript show her careful revision and rethinking of individual words, lines, and scenes. But the final narrative also benefited from the careful, exacting comments of Michael di Capua, her editor. He focused on specific problems in the text as well as language that might be anachronistic in 1884. Both author and editor worked diligently to develop this novel, which is part fantasy, part historical fiction. Trained as an artist, Natalie Babbitt even painted the watercolor for the jacket of the book to create the feeling and mood that she wanted.

Unlike many classics, *Tuck Everlasting* was thoroughly praised by reviewers, getting accolade after accolade in print. But it failed to receive any major children's book prize, including the Newbery or the National Book Award. What the book has captured over the years is the devotion of teachers and students who find it an ideal book for classroom or family discussion. Should Winnie Foster drink the water? Should she become immortal? Would long life be a gift or a curse? With these questions to be answered, *Tuck Everlasting* remains a children's book that excites young readers and has a deeper resonance for adults. Personally, if I had only one children's book to take to my desert island, it would be *Tuck Everlasting*.

Behind the Attic Wall

....

By Sylvia Cassedy (1930–1989)
Published in 1983 by T. Y. Crowell
Ages 11 to 12   315 pages

An unlovable and unloving orphan, Maggie is sent to live with her great-aunts. Only Maggie's own imagination and an occasional visit from her eccentric uncle make the dreary household bearable. Hearing rustlings and voices, Maggie explores the deserted rooms of the house. Finally she discovers a hidden room inhabited by two dolls who live a clandestine, secret life. As she participates in their activities, Maggie changes; she uses her rich fantasy life to gain the strength to survive and grow. A true preadolescent, she learns to cope with rejection and self-acceptance. The book explores the power of caretaking to alter the life of a troubled human being. After cherishing the dolls, Maggie can sing a song, join in a game, cry over a death, and finally say "I love you."

Fifteen years after she published a book of haikus for young readers, Sylvia Cassedy finished this haunting, original work of fiction and sent it to a friend of her first editor. In awe of Cassedy's talent, Marilyn Kriney saw a manuscript, fully formed and beautifully crafted, that needed very little alteration. Before submitting her book, Cassedy had worked and reworked her own writing, aiming for perfection and subtle nuance.

Although many at Crowell expressed a great deal of concern over the commercial prospects of such a long manuscript, Kriney knew that it needed to be published in its entirety. She also defended the work when some raised their eyebrows at its ambiguous ending.

However, it is precisely that ending that first won the praise of critics and makes the book so powerful. One can read *Behind the Attic Wall* either as sunny and optimistic or as a devastating, three-handkerchief book. Each reader, and each reading, brings a different interpretation. Hence, for two decades this doll story has pulled a devoted group of readers behind the attic wall — delighting in what they find there and in the author's deft exploration of a child's inner, imaginative world.

Catherine, Called Birdy

By Karen Cushman (b. 1941)
Published in 1994 by Clarion Books
Newbery Honor Book
Ages 11 to 12   212 pages

Described in a series of journal entries for the year 1290, Catherine, called Birdy because she keeps caged birds in her room, gives the reader a vivid sense of her life as the daughter of an impoverished knight. "My mother seeks to make me a fine lady — dumb, docile, and accomplished — so I must take lady-lessons and keep my mouth closed. . . . My father, the toad, conspires to sell me like a cheese to some lack-wit seeking a wife." An inventive fourteen-year-old, Birdy attempts to find creative ways to avoid marriage — such as blackening her teeth. Cushman immerses her readers completely in the setting; they experience the tastes, smell the odors, and even hear the archaic swear words of the era.

Manuscripts of great books connect with publishers in a variety of ways; *Catherine, Called Birdy* was delivered in an elevator. Beginning her writing career rather late in life, Karen Cushman, who lived in California, had no idea how to get her manuscript published and placed it in the hands of an agent in New York, Jim Levine. Levine found out that Dorothy Briley, a respected publisher of children's books, lived in his apartment complex. So he stalked her, waiting for a moment when they could be alone together and he could talk to her about Cushman's book.

One evening, as Briley stepped into the elevator, Levine rushed in behind her. He introduced himself and brought forth the manuscript. Briley thanked him for the gift, made sure it included a return address, and said good-bye. But rather than calling security, she looked at the book and turned it over to the editor Dinah Stevenson the next morning. Stevenson, upon reading the text, "felt the hair on her arms stand up." Even though no one was publishing Medieval historical fiction in the early 1990s, Stevenson fell in love with the character and story and decided that she had to give the book a chance.

Millions of readers are grateful that she did. They have grown to appreciate Birdy, who is assertive, imaginative, stubborn, brave, funny, and determined to be her own person. Although she lived in the Middle Ages, Birdy has enchanted contemporary young girls — and boys have also found her much to their liking.

Johnny Tremain

By Esther Forbes (1891–1967)
Published in 1943 by Houghton Mifflin
Newbery Medal
Ages 11 to 12   256 pages

A descendant of Samuel Adams, the organizer of the Sons of Liberty, Esther Forbes believed herself to be as "steeped in Colonial New Englandiana as pickle is in brine." Although a writer from childhood on, she suffered from nearsightedness and something resembling dyslexia; consequently her spelling and grammar remained atrocious all of her life. She once confessed that the dash was the only punctuation she ever mastered.

But her inattention to these details did not prevent her from pursuing a life in books, first in publishing at Houghton Mifflin as the assistant to the editor in chief. Because her spelling left something to be desired, she read manuscripts rather than typing letters. However, reading other writers' manuscripts made her long to write her own.

A meticulous researcher, she began working on a historical novel about Paul Revere. In the process, she abandoned the novel format and undertook, with the help of her mother, a biography of Revere instead. *Paul Revere and the World He Lived In* won the Pulitzer Prize and established Forbes's reputation as a historian and writer.

While working on the book, Forbes gained an appreciation of the role of apprentices in the fight for independence. On the night of Paul Revere's famous ride, one British stable boy shared valuable information with another stable boy who was loyal to the Americans. Forbes went on to construct her own story around a silversmith's apprentice, who badly burns his right hand while crafting a basin handle. Spanning two years in the life of young orphan Johnny Tremain, the book presents his search for a new trade and his growing involvement with the Sons of Liberty, as he and his friends advance the cause of the Americans. Because she had so thoroughly researched the time period and background, Forbes got inside the story and brings to life the characters of Paul Revere, Sam Adams, and John Hancock. Although Forbes knew little about writing for children, she decided to create a character "as I thought he ought to be, not perfect, but with an ordinary mixture of good and bad in him."

Finishing the book in the spring of 1942, Forbes sent it to Harcourt Brace and then took a much-needed vacation. However, she returned to find that the manuscript had been completely altered by one of Harcourt's editors. Consequently, she pulled the book and offered it to Houghton Mifflin's Grace Hogarth. Although thrilled to read a manuscript by such a fine writer, Hogarth was shocked by the errors of spelling and grammar. When she mentioned to Forbes that the manuscript needed cleaning up, Forbes laughed and said, "My editor always deals with that." Not only did her editor have to deal with her sloppy manuscripts, but Forbes drove two aging proofreaders at the Riverside Press, which printed *Johnny Tremain*, absolutely crazy with her lack of attention to spelling and punctuation.

Forbes saw parallels between *Johnny Tremain*, a book about the Revolutionary War, published during World War II, and her own times. As she said in her Newbery acceptance speech, "In peace times countries are apt to look upon their boys under twenty as mere children and (for better or worse) to treat them as such. When war comes, these boys are suddenly asked to play their part as men. . . . I wanted . . . to show the boys and girls of today how difficult were those other children's lives by modern standards. . . . They were not allowed to be children very long."

From the beginning, reviewers and readers embraced *Johnny Tremain*, and it has sold 5 million copies in paperback. Forbes explores complex issues — struggling with disability, taking responsibility for one's actions, coping with death, giving oneself wholeheartedly to a just cause, and showing true heroism. The book's content, Forbes's incredible knowledge of the period, and her mastery of character development make *Johnny Tremain* one of the finest historical novels ever written for the young.

Anne Frank: The Diary of a Young Girl

By Anne Frank (1929–1945)
Published in 1952 by Doubleday
Ages 11 to 12   283 pages

Born into an upper-class Jewish family in Frankfurt, Anne Frank moved with her family to Amsterdam in 1933. But in 1941 when the Nazis began rounding up Amsterdam's Jews, Otto Frank and his business partners prepared a secret hiding place in rooms at the top and back of their office building on Prinsengracht

Canal. In the secret annex, they were joined by Mr. and Mrs. Van Pelz (renamed Van Daan in Anne's diary) and their son, along with Albert Dussel, a dentist.

On June 12, 1942, Anne celebrated her thirteenth birthday and received a clothbound diary, which she used to record her feelings and thoughts until August 1, 1944. Through her diary, we learn about life in the annex as the group remained hidden and virtually imprisoned for two years. In August 1944, the Nazis discovered this hiding place; in March 1945 Anne died of typhoid fever in the Bergen-Belsen concentration camp. Of the eight inhabitants of the annex, only Otto Frank survived. When he returned to Amsterdam, Anne's writings, which had been saved in a desk, came into his hands. Surprised by the depth of her statements, he typed a copy, which at first circulated among friends.

Motivated by a strong desire to write, Frank disclosed her thoughts and feelings to the diary. She named it Kitty and wrote her entries in the form of letters. But as an ordinary girl living in extraordinary times, her voice speaks for millions of people destroyed in World War II. This diary serves as a candid self-portrait, a picture of domestic life, an account of people threatened with death, a depiction of the problems common to young adults, and an examination of moral issues. The writing also shows the triumph of the human spirit in terrible times. "It's a wonder that I haven't abandoned all my ideals; they seem so absurd and impractical. Yet I cling to them because I still believe, in spite of everything, that people are truly good at heart. It's utterly impossible for me to build my life on a foundation of chaos, suffering and death. I see the world being slowly transformed into a wilderness, I hear the approaching thunder that, one day, will destroy us too, I feel the suffering of millions. And yet, when I look up at the sky, I somehow feel that everything will change for the better, that this cruelty too will end, and that peace and tranquility will return once more."

In Germany, several publishers turned down the diary, until eventually an article about its existence drew the attention of a publisher, who at first issued only fifteen hundred copies in 1947. Five years later, after the book had been rejected by many houses, the English and American editions appeared. Eleanor Roosevelt in her introduction called *The Diary of a Young Girl* "one of the wisest and most moving commentaries on war and its impact on human beings that I have ever read." With her sincere words she introduced the most important children's book of the 1950s to an audience of young readers. Although critics at first were chary of the difficult emotional content, by the end of 1952 young readers had convinced them of the diary's power and ability to speak to them. Edited by Anne's father, this 1952 edition did not include a great deal of material he felt to be inappropriate, such as Anne's catty words about others. For those who want to learn more about the diary and Anne, a longer definitive edition, with much previously unpublished material, has been translated, and *Anne Frank: Beyond the Diary* includes photographs of the diary itself, Anne, and her family.

For over fifty years, the book has continued to teach children about the horror of the war, as seen through the eyes of a young woman. With more than 15 million readers worldwide, this memoir, drawn from a simple diary, in the end has fulfilled one of Anne Frank's greatest dreams: "I want to go on living even after my death!"

Out of the Dust

By Karen Hesse (b. 1952)
Published in 1997 by Scholastic
Newbery Medal
Ages 11 to 12   227 pages

When Karen Hesse took a road trip from Vermont to Colorado with author Liza Ketchum, she fell in love with the Kansas plains and began thinking about life in that region. Later, while working on a picture book, *Come on, Rain!*, Hesse began to wonder why a child would desire rain. That question brought her thoughts to the prairie again, to a time and place when people longed for rain. Set in the Oklahoma Dust Bowl in the 1930s, *Out of the Dust* concentrates on the protagonist, fourteen-year-old Billie

Jo. When her mother dies in a tragic accident, the lives of Billie Jo and her father change forever.

For *Out of the Dust*, Hesse conducted extensive research in newspapers of the period, carefully observing the daily weather reports. As she wrote, her narrative evolved. In the original manuscript, Billy Jo wrote poetry and played the piano, but that dual talent seemed inconsistent with the training and life she had lived. Because Hesse wanted to show a child who experienced a simple life, she decided that free verse would be the ideal form in which to convey that sparseness. She selected every word, every line break, with care — from the opening sentence to the final "And I stretch my fingers over the keys, / and I play."

The photo of young Lucille Burroughs on the book jacket first appeared in Walker Evans's *Let Us Now Praise Famous Men*. In searching for a cover illustration, Hesse's editor, Brenda Bowen, found this photograph and decided that it perfectly fit the mood and feeling of the story. Hesse thought so too: that same photograph had actually been in her studio as she wrote the book.

Many authors have the ability to create books quite popular with children; some have the ability to write complex books not always accessible to the young. A few, like Karen Hesse, can combine exceptional quality with great appeal to children. In all her books, she tackles subjects of great significance and does not hesitate to examine them honestly. In *Out of the Dust*, the heat, the longing, the anguish, the pain of living, and the healing from tragedy have all been presented to readers in spare, haunting verse.

A Wizard of Earthsea

Written by Ursula K. Le Guin (b. 1929)
Illustrated by Ruth Robbins (b. 1917)
Published in 1968 by Parnassus Press
Ages 11 to 12   183 pages

An author of adult science-fiction novels, Ursula Le Guin never expected to write for another audience. But in 1967,

Herbert Schein, the publisher at a small California house, wrote to Le Guin, asking her if she would consider creating a children's book. The resulting book, *A Wizard of Earthsea*, gave Le Guin a chance to explore a coming-of-age story using a fantasy framework.

Taking place on an island, set in time several hundred years ago, *A Wizard of Earthsea* presents a community that views magic very seriously and protects it. A young goatherd, Ged, undertakes a journey to become a wizard; he achieves this role through formal education at the wizards' academy and through his experiences of the world. But his own pride and ambition prove far more danger-ous than dragons or evil sorcerers. These character defects cause him to summon from the darkness a shadow that almost destroys him. In one of the most satisfying endings in all fantasy novels for children, Ged must ultimately turn to face this shadow, name it — and merge with it.

Le Guin decided to go against all fantasy convention when she made her villains white-skinned and her heroes black or brown. Although she meant this device to be a strike against racial bigotry, she also wanted to subvert the entire European heroic tradition of fantasy. Ged stands as an outsider to that tradition.

The novel quickly caught the attention of the children's book community and won the prestigious Boston Globe–Horn Book Award. Le Guin would go on to craft other books in the Earthsea saga and win countless prizes for both her adult and her children's writing. But *A Wizard of Earthsea* remains her greatest contribu-tion to children's literature. It combines a superb quest or journey story with a psychological reality — learning to face the darkness inside. Not only has it excited generations of children, it has pro-foundly affected the next generation of children's book editors, no-tably Arthur Levine, who later published another account of a wiz-ards' academy, *Harry Potter and the Sorcerer's Stone*.

The Giver

....

By Lois Lowry (b. 1937)
Published in 1993 by Houghton Mifflin
Newbery Medal
Ages 11 to 12   208 pages

In 1993, Lois Lowry found herself frequently visiting a nursing home. Her mother and father were residents in separate sections. Going blind, her mother would relate tales of childhood. Although in better physical condition, her father slowly lost his memory. While there, Lowry started to think about the importance of memory.

In the same time period, she took her nine-year-old grandson for a Swan Boat ride in Boston's Public Garden. He said to her, "Have you ever noticed that when people think they are manipulating ducks, actually ducks are manipulating people?" This comment haunted her, and she began wondering what kind of world her grandchildren would inherit.

Dedicating this book to "all the children to whom we entrust the future," Lowry began writing a novel about a future utopia. But after a while she saw the dark side of the world she had been creating. Eventually, she realized — as readers of *The Giver* grow to understand — that she had created a dystopian novel.

Set in a futuristic world that would appear to have solved all problems — poverty, inequality, loneliness, and old age — *The Giver* chronicles the coming of age of twelve-year-old Jonas. Jonas becomes an apprentice to the Giver, the keeper of all the memories that the community has abandoned to achieve its current stability. In the process, Jonas begins to question the choices made by his community and what it means for his future. One of literature's most impassioned young protagonists, Jonas must ultimately face the inadequacies and hypocrisies of his parents' generation.

From lighthearted tales about Anastasia Krupnik and her brother, Sam, to the beautiful cadences of *Autumn Street*, a more serious autobiographical work, Lois Lowry had always shown an amazing range in her writing. In *The Giver*, her twenty-first novel for children, she emphasized philosophy and plot. From the opening sentence, "It was almost December, and Jonas was beginning to be frightened," readers get pulled along in the sweep of the narrative.

Some critics and even Lowry's longtime editor, Walter Lorraine, expressed concern over the ending of the book. However, reviewers who supported the book applauded its ambiguity, which allows each reader to determine the fate of Jonas: "For the first time, he heard something that he knew to be music. He heard people singing. . . . But perhaps it was only an echo." Lowry, however, always maintained that she intended the ending to be optimistic. In a subsequent book, *Gathering Blue*, Jonas makes a cameo appearance, confirming his survival.

A photographer as well as a writer, Lowry had worked on an article about the painter Carl Nelson, who had a wonderful sense of color but became blind in later years. For this piece she shot a mesmerizing portrait of him. She kept the photograph in her studio and realized when hunting for a jacket image that it would be perfect for *The Giver*.

From the moment of its publication the book, provocative, moving, and haunting, emerged as an ideal story to read and share, whether in parent-child book groups or in the classroom. Now with 3.5 million copies in print, *The Giver* has proved to be not only one of the greatest novels of the 1990s for children but also one of the greatest science-fiction novels for young readers of all time.

Unflinching in her conviction that young readers can face issues of great importance, Lois Lowry wrote a book demonstrating something she strongly believes: "Pain, too, is a gift of great value. It is what makes us human."

Roll of Thunder, Hear My Cry

··

By Mildred Taylor (b. 1943)
Published in 1976 by Dial Books
Newbery Medal
Ages 11 to 12   276 pages

Mildred Taylor had unsuccessfully tried to reconstruct her family history, and then she heard about a contest sponsored by the Council on Interracial Books. After attempting to write a piece using the voice of her father, she shifted the storytelling to a young girl, Cassie Logan, four days before the contest deadline. That shift and the resulting book, *Song of the Trees*, won the contest for Taylor. On the way home from the award ceremony, Taylor heard from her father and uncle the story of a black boy who had broken into a store and how he was saved from lynching. Taylor began to tell that saga, one that she thought might make an adult book.

It turned out to be a book many children's literature critics consider the most important historical novel in the latter half of the twentieth century. Like Laura Ingalls Wilder before her, Mildred Taylor wrote family history — but Taylor's family history told of the problems of segregation and of the triumph and determination of blacks to overcome their plight.

In *Roll of Thunder, Hear My Cry*, the Logans, a proud black family living on their own land in Mississippi, experience all the racial prejudice of the 1930s. The children receive poor, hand-me-down textbooks; they see the nightriders, who come to burn and terrorize blacks. They have to fight to keep their land. But they are such worthy protagonists that readers, no matter what their skin color or heritage, find themselves on the side of the Logans, battling prejudice with them. One of Taylor's greatest strengths as a novelist lies in her ability to show racial prejudice from the viewpoint of a child.

Taylor continued the saga of the Logan family in several books: *Let the Circle Be Unbroken*, *The Gold Cadillac*, *The Friendship*, *The Road to Memphis*, *Mississippi Bridge*, *The Well*, and *The Land*. Those who become intrigued by these characters — Cassie, Stacey, Little Man, David — can follow their stories through these volumes. In *The Land,* Taylor discusses her own obsession with buying a piece of land. She sacrificed and sold many items, including her house, furniture, and jewelry, to keep her land. Eventually, she sold the typewriter on which she had written *Roll of Thunder, Hear My Cry.*

In the 1970s, Mildred Taylor emerged as one of the most important voices in children's books. A classroom favorite, *Roll of Thunder, Hear My Cry* explores a period of history quite unknown by today's young readers. Now past its twentieth-fifth anniversary, the novel has become the most popular children's book written by a black writer, selling close to 3 million copies in paperback.

The Hobbit

....

By J.R.R. Tolkien (1892–1973)
Published in 1938 by Houghton Mifflin
Ages 11 to 12   330 pages

In 1917, J.R.R. Tolkien began chronicling the legends of the First Age of Middle-earth, a mythological epic eventually called *The Silmarillion.* He would go back to the saga again and again, writing and rewriting. For Middle-earth, he even invented elvish languages.

Then one day, as the Oxford professor graded exam papers, he found a blank page with no writing on it. Tolkien took up his pen and wrote, "In a hole in the ground there lived a hobbit" and then decided he'd better figure out what hobbits were. As he played with the idea, Tolkien envisioned creatures of small imagination but great courage — the kind of courage he had seen fighting in the trenches in World War I. Around 1930, he began writing the story of one such hobbit, Bilbo Baggins, and told tales about hobbits at night to his three sons. But although the saga began as personal entertainment, eventually Bilbo strayed into the rich history of Middle-earth that Tolkien had already created.

Through a student of Tolkien's, the existence of *The Hobbit* came to the attention of a publisher, Allen and Unwin, and editors pursued him for the story. In 1936, when the completed typescript was delivered, Stanley Unwin, the chairman of the publishing company, asked his young son, Rayner, to read the book and write a report on it. The critique ended with this opinion: "This book, with the help of maps, does not need any illustrations. . . . It is good and should appeal to all children between the ages of 5 and 9." Young master Unwin — who was ten — was paid a shilling for his views.

Unwin Senior, whom Tolkien felt looked exactly like one of his dwarfs, believed that the book needed illustrations, and asked Tolkien to draw and paint some pictures. Tolkien also designed a jacket, which he decorated with runes. *The Hobbit* contained two maps. One, showing Wilderland and the places where Bilbo's adventures happened, was designed as an endpaper. Tolkien wanted the other map in the first chapter of the book, at the point where Gandalf the wizard shows the map to Bilbo and the dwarfs. Tolkien had even hoped that some of the lettering on the map would be printed using "invisible ink." However, the publishers found this idea too expensive, and, eventually, the map — with all the letters completely visible — appeared as the front endpaper.

In *The Hobbit*, Bilbo Baggins, a comfort-loving, ordinary, and unlikely hero, joins a band of dwarfs, gathered with the aid of Gandalf. They set out from Bilbo's home to seek treasure hoarded by Smaug the dragon. As they experience various adventures, and escape spiders, goblins, and the dragon itself, Bilbo grows in courage, strength, and wisdom. Along the way, he retrieves from a creature of the swamps, the Gollum, a magic ring that makes him invisible but also possesses greater powers than he knows.

The book instantly proved both a commercial and a critical success, and Tolkien's publishers asked for another Hobbit book. *The Hobbit* begins with a chapter called "An Unexpected Party"; the new book, *The Fellowship of the Ring*, opened with a chapter entitled "A Long-Expected Party," in which Bilbo used his magic ring to disappear at his own eleventy-first birthday party. The ring turned out to be one of several rings of great power forged by the dark lord Sauron — referred to in *The Hobbit* as the Necromancer — in order to control the people of Middle-earth. In 1951, while completing the Lord of the Rings trilogy, Tolkien went back to make significant changes to *The Hobbit,* particularly Chapter V, "Riddles in the Dark," to bring the book in line with later events. Someone who worked toward narrative perfection, Tolkien made minor alterations to his texts all his life.

Although many fine heroic fantasies have been created for children, *The Hobbit* stands as the precursor to them all. At the end of the book, Gandalf tells Bilbo: "You are a very fine person, Mr. Baggins, and I am very fond of you; but you are only quite a little fellow in a wide world after all." Yet as millions upon millions of readers, recently enlarged by a series of popular movie adaptations of the books, have found Bilbo and his cousin Frodo Baggins, the world of the hobbit has expanded each year since its creation. Consequently, this little fellow, Bilbo Baggins, has played a major role in the canon of children's literature.

Homecoming

By Cynthia Voigt (b. 1942)
Published in 1981 by Atheneum Publishers
Ages 11 to 12   372 pages

R ealistic fiction usually ages badly and does not stand the test of time. Little of it stays around for lengthy periods, precisely because conventions change and so does dialect. Only an author who can move this fiction to a more universal sphere seems to have the ability to remain in print over time. Like Katherine Paterson, author of *Bridge to Terabithia,* Cynthia Voigt proves to be one of those writers.

An English teacher turned writer, Cynthia Voigt one day saw a car full of children, left alone in a parking lot, and wondered what would happen to them if the adult in charge failed to return.

In *Homecoming,* the four Tillerman children are abandoned by their mentally ill mother in a car at a shopping mall in Connecticut. Thirteen-year-old Dicey, practical and responsible, an adult before her years, takes over the care of James, Maybeth, and Sammy. With limited funds, the four set out on a dangerous journey walking down U.S. Route 1 to Crisfield, Maryland, where they know their grandmother lives. They must use their wits, strength, and resourcefulness, and make moral choices, to reach their final destination. In a believable ending, although their grandmother welcomes them reluctantly, she tentatively agrees to share her life with these four needy children.

Even now a long novel, the first version of the book had twice as many pages. Voigt went on to write six other books about the Tillermans, including *Dicey's Song*, winner of the Newbery Medal. Readers of that book will still want to begin with *Homecoming* — a book with vivid descriptions, a strong sense of place, and memorable characters.

Although containing a fast-paced plot with a great deal of suspense, the book deals with the pain of death, separation, and poverty. But it ultimately tells the story of the survival, and resilience, of four memorable children and their grandmother. Cynthia Voigt always said that Dicey was the child she would like to have been and Gram the kind of lady she would want to be — and child and adult readers of the Tillerman saga often feel the same way.

**Beyond the 100 Best
Bibliography
Reading Journal
Index**

Beyond the 100 Best

The books in bold are those that I've discussed in *100 Best Books for Children;* these familiar titles can be used to locate others. All the books on this list maintain a high degree of excellence. Ages are suggestions only. The individual child is the real criterion.

Preschool Books   Birth to Age 2

Goodnight Moon by Margaret Wise Brown
Mr. Gumpy's Outing by John Burningham
The Very Hungry Caterpillar by Eric Carle
Freight Train by Donald Crews
Good Dog, Carl by Alexandra Day
Color Zoo by Lois Ehlert
Sheila Rae's Peppermint Stick by Kevin Henkes
Where's Spot by Eric Hill
Black on White by Tana Hoban
Rosie's Walk by Pat Hutchins
Whose Mouse Are You? by Robert Kraus
The Carrot Seed by Ruth Krauss
Brown Bear, Brown Bear, What Do You See? by Bill Martin, Jr.
Tickle Tickle by Helen Oxenbury
One Duck Stuck by Phyllis Root
We're Going on a Bear Hunt by Michael Rosen
Have You Seen My Duckling? by Nancy Tafuri
Max's First Words by Rosemary Wells
Don't Let the Pigeon Drive the Bus by Mo Willems
"More More More," Said the Baby by Vera B. Williams

Alphabet Books
Anno's Alphabet by Mitsumasa Anno
Jambo Means Hello by Tom Feelings
Pigs from A to Z by Arthur Geisert
Aardvarks, Disembark! by Ann Jonas
Chicka Chicka Boom Boom by Bill Martin, Jr., and John Archambault
Brian Wildsmith's ABC by Brian Wildsmith

Counting Books

Anno's Counting Book by Mitsumasa Anno
Ten, Nine, Eight by Molly Bang
Ten Black Dots by Donald Crews
Mojo Means One: A Swahili Counting Book by Muriel and Tom Feelings
Pigs from 1 to 10 by Arthur Geisert
1, 2, 3 by Tana Hoban
One Hunter by Pat Hutchins
Who's Counting? by Nancy Tafuri

Nursery Rhymes

The Mother Goose Treasury by Raymond Briggs
The Random House Book of Mother Goose by Arnold Lobel
My Very First Mother Goose by Iona Opie
The Tall Book of Mother Goose by Feodor Rojankovsky
London Bridge Is Falling Down by Peter Spier
Father Fox's Pennyrhymes by Clyde Watson
The Real Mother Goose by Blanche Fisher Wright

Picture Books   Ages 2 to 8

Miss Nelson Is Missing! by Harry Allard
Madeline by Ludwig Bemelmans
The Snowman by Raymond Briggs
Arthur's Birthday by Marc Brown
The Color Kittens by Margaret Wise Brown
Gorilla by Anthony Browne
The Story of Babar by Jean de Brunhoff
The Little House by Virginia Lee Burton
Mike Mulligan and His Steam Shovel by Virginia Lee Burton
The Tub People by Pam Conrad
Miss Rumphius by Barbara Cooney
Click Clack Moo: Cows That Type by Doreen Cronin
Andy and the Lion by James Daugherty
Bark, George by Jules Feiffer
The Story About Ping by Marjorie Flack
Lunch by Denise Fleming
Corduroy by Don Freeman
Millions of Cats by Wanda Gág
The Shrinking of Treehorn by Florence Parry Heide
Kitten's First Full Moon by Kevin Henkes

Lilly's Purple Plastic Purse by Kevin Henkes
Bread and Jam for Frances by Russell Hoban
Angelina Ballerina by Katherine Holabird
Swamp Angel by Anne Isaacs
Harold and the Purple Crayon by Crockett Johnson
The Snowy Day by Ezra Jack Keats
Leo the Late Bloomer by Robert Kraus
A Hole Is to Dig by Ruth Krauss
The Story of Ferdinand by Munro Leaf
Swimmy by Leo Lionni
George and Martha by James Marshall
Lottie's New Beach Towel by Petra Mathers
Make Way for Ducklings by Robert McCloskey
Martha Speaks by Susan Meddaugh
Pink and Say by Patricia Polacco
The Tale of Peter Rabbit by Beatrix Potter
Yo! Yes? by Chris Raschka
Officer Buckle and Gloria by Peggy Rathmann
Curious George by H. A. Rey
The Relatives Came by Cynthia Rylant
Math Curse by Jon Scieszka
The True Story of the 3 Little Pigs by Jon Scieszka
Where the Wild Things Are by Maurice Sendak
And to Think That I Saw It on Mulberry Street by Dr. Seuss
Horton Hatches the Egg by Dr. Seuss
No, David! by David Shannon
Caps for Sale by Esphyr Slobodkina
Doctor De Soto by William Steig
Sylvester and the Magic Pebble by William Steig
The Gardener by Sarah Stewart
Many Moons by James Thurber
Do Not Open by Brinton Turkle
Crictor by Tomi Ungerer
The Three Robbers by Tomi Ungerer
The Polar Express by Chris Van Allsburg
Alexander and the Terrible, Horrible, No Good, Very Bad Day by Judith
   Viorst
Ira Sleeps Over by Bernard Waber
The Three Pigs by David Wiesner
Tuesday by David Wiesner
A Chair for My Mother by Vera Williams
Crow Boy by Taro Yashima

It Could Always Be Worse by Margot Zemach
The Judge by Harve Zemach
Harry the Dirty Dog by Gene Zion
William's Doll by Charlotte Zolotow

Books for Beginning Readers   Ages 5 to 7

Small Wolf by Nathaniel Benchley
Bedtime for Frances by Russell Hoban
Frog and Toad Are Friends by Arnold Lobel
Little Bear by Else Holmelund Minarik
Amelia Bedelia series by Peggy Parish
Henry and Mudge by Cynthia Rylant
Winnie All Day Long by Leda Schubert
The Cat in the Hat by Dr. Seuss
Nate the Great series by Marjorie Sharmat

Books for Young Readers   Ages 7 to 9

Mr. Popper's Penguins by Richard and Florence Atwater
Tales of a Fourth-Grade Nothing by Judy Blume
The Enormous Egg by Oliver Butterworth
Henry Huggins series by Beverly Cleary
The Mouse on the Motorcycle by Beverly Cleary
Ramona the Pest by Beverly Cleary
The Courage of Sarah Noble by Alice Dalgliesh
The Hundred Dresses by Eleanor Estes
Great Brain series by John D. Fitzgerald
My Father's Dragon by Ruth Stiles Gannett
Stone Fox by John Gardiner
Misty of Chincoteague by Marguerite Henry
Betsy-Tacy by Maud Hart Lovelace
Mrs. Piggle-Wiggle by Betty MacDonald
Sarah, Plain and Tall by Patricia MacLachlan
Encyclopedia Brown series by Donald J. Sobol
Little House in the Big Woods by Laura Ingalls Wilder

Books for Middle Readers   Ages 8 to 11

On My Honor by Marion Dane Bauer
The House with the Clock in Its Walls by John Bellairs

Summer of the Swans by Betsy Byars
Ordinary Jack by Helen Cresswell
Gone-Away Lake by Elizabeth Enright
Moffat series by Eleanor Estes
Harriet the Spy by Louise Fitzhugh
Humbug Mountain by Sid Fleischman
Joey Pigza series by Jack Gantos
My Side of the Mountain by Jean Craighead George
Hoot by Carl Hiaasen
My Louisiana Sky by Kimberly Willis Holt
From the Mixed-up Files of Mrs. Basil E. Frankweiler by E. L. Konigsburg
Pippi Longstocking by Astrid Lindgren
Anastasia Krupnik series by Lois Lowry
Homer Price by Robert McCloskey
The Pushcart War by Jean Merrill
Anne of Green Gables by Lucy Maud Montgomery
Bridge to Terabithia by Katherine Paterson
The Great Gilly Hopkins by Katherine Paterson
The Westing Game by Ellen Raskin
Henry Reed series by Keith Robertson
The Best Christmas Pageant Ever by Barbara Robinson
Holes by Louis Sachar
Stargirl by Jerry Spinelli
Ballet Shoes by Noel Streatfeild

Animal/Horse Stories
Black Stallion series by Walter Farley
King of the Wind by Marguerite Henry
Smoky, the Cowhorse by Will James
Owls in the Family by Farley Mowat
Rascal by Sterling North
My Friend Flicka by Mary O'Hara
The Yearling by Marjorie Kinnan Rawlings

Dog Stories
Sounder by William Armstrong
The Incredible Journey by Sheila Burnford
Because of Winn-Dixie by Kate DiCamillo
Old Yeller by Fred Gipson
Lassie Come-Home by Eric Knight
The Call of the Wild by Jack London
Shiloh by Phyllis Reynolds Naylor
Where the Red Fern Grows by Wilson Rawls

Fantasy

The Wolves of Willoughby Chase by Joan Aiken
Chronicles of Prydain series by Lloyd Alexander
Tuck Everlasting by Natalie Babbitt
The Children of Green Knowe by L. M. Boston
The Secret Garden by Frances Hodgson Burnett
Behind the Attic Wall by Sylvia Cassedy
The Dark Is Rising by Susan Cooper
The BFG by Roald Dahl
Half Magic by Edward Eager
Inkheart by Cornelia Funke
The Wind in the Willows by Kenneth Grahame
The Mouse and His Child by Russell Hoban
Finn Family Moomintroll by Tove Jansson
The Animal Family by Randall Jarrell
The Phantom Tollbooth by Norton Juster
The Gammage Cup by Carol Kendall
The Diamond in the Window by Jane Langton
A Wizard of Earthsea by Ursula K. Le Guin
Ella Enchanted by Gail Carson Levine
The Lion, the Witch, and the Wardrobe by C. S. Lewis
The Story of Dr. Dolittle by Hugh Lofting
Winnie-the-Pooh by A. A. Milne
Borrowers series by Mary Norton
Tom's Midnight Garden by Philippa Pearce
The Twenty-One Balloons by William Pène du Bois
The Perilous Gard by Elizabeth Marie Pope
Freaky Friday by Mary Rodgers
Harry Potter and the Sorcerer's Stone by J. K. Rowling
The Little Prince by Antoine de Saint-Exupéry
Unfortunate Events series by Lemony Snicket
The Hobbit by J.R.R. Tolkien
Mary Poppins by P. L. Travers
The Sword in the Stone by T. H. White

Animal Fantasy

A Bear Called Paddington by Michael Bond
Freddy the Pig series by Walter R. Brooks
Redwall by Brian Jacques
Babe: The Gallant Pig by Dick King-Smith
Rabbit Hill by Robert Lawson

The Cricket in Times Square by George Selden
Charlotte's Web by E. B. White

Historical Fiction (Ages 10 to 14)
The True Confessions of Charlotte Doyle by Avi
Caddie Woodlawn by Carol Ryrie Brink
Al Capone Does My Shirts by Gennifer Choldenko
My Brother Sam Is Dead by James and Christopher Collier
Catherine, Called Birdy by Karen Cushman
Johnny Tremain by Esther Forbes
Out of the Dust by Karen Hesse
Across Five Aprils by Irene Hunt
Because My Name Was Keoko by Linda Sue Park
The Kite Fighters by Linda Sue Park
A Long Way from Chicago by Richard Peck
The Teacher's Funeral by Richard Peck
The Light in the Forest by Conrad Richter
The Witch of Blackbird Pond by Elizabeth George Speare
Jeremy Visick by David Wiseman

Science Fiction (Ages 10 to 14)
Ender's Game by Orson Scott Card
The White Mountains by John Christopher
Eva by Peter Dickinson
The City of Ember by Jean DuPrau
Enchantress from the Stars by Sylvia Louise Engdahl
The Ear, the Eye and the Arm by Nancy Farmer
Devil on My Back by Monica Hughes
A Wrinkle in Time by Madeleine L'Engle
The Giver by Lois Lowry
Mrs. Frisby and the Rats of NIMH by Robert C. O'Brien
Mortal Engines by Philip Reeve
Interstellar Pig by William Sleator

Survival Stories
Julie of the Wolves by Jean Craighead George
My Side of the Mountain by Jean Craighead George
Z for Zachariah by Robert C. O'Brien
Island of the Blue Dolphins by Scott O'Dell
Wreckers by Iain Lawrence
Hatchet by Gary Paulsen
Call It Courage by Armstrong Sperry

Books for Older Readers   Ages 11 to 14

Skellig by David Almond
Speak by Laurie Halse Anderson
Feed by M. T. Anderson
Tangerine by Edward Bloor
The Moves Make the Man by Bruce Brooks
The Goats by Brock Cole
The Chocolate War by Robert Cormier
Stotan! by Chris Crutcher
A Northern Light by Jennifer Donnelly
One-Eyed Cat by Paula Fox
The Outsiders by S. E. Hinton
Silent to the Bone by E. L. Konigsburg
One Fat Summer by Robert Lipsyte
Beauty by Robin McKinley
The Hero and the Crown by Robin McKinley
Fallen Angels by Walter Dean Myers
Monster by Walter Dean Myers
Zel by Donna Jo Napoli
The Ghost Belonged to Me by Richard Peck
His Dark Materials series by Philip Pullman
Shane by Jack Shaefer
Maniac Magee by Jerry Spinelli
Homecoming by Cynthia Voigt
The Pigman by Paul Zindel

Books for Various Ages

Classics
Little Women by Louisa May Alcott
The Fairy Tales of Hans Christian Andersen by Hans Christian
    Andersen
The Wonderful Wizard of Oz by L. Frank Baum
Alice's Adventures in Wonderland by Lewis Carroll
The Adventures of Pinocchio by Carlo Collodi
The Jungle Book by Rudyard Kipling
The Boy's King Arthur by Sidney Lanier
Five Children and It by E. Nesbit
The Railway Children by E. Nesbit
The Merry Adventures of Robin Hood by Howard Pyle

Swallows and Amazons by Arthur Ransome
Heidi by Johanna Spyri
Kidnapped by Robert Louis Stevenson
Treasure Island by Robert Louis Stevenson
The Adventures of Huckleberry Finn by Mark Twain
The Adventures of Tom Sawyer by Mark Twain

Information Books
Sir Walter Ralegh and the Quest for El Dorado by Marc Aronson
The Magic School Bus at the Waterworks by Joanna Cole
Anne Frank: The Diary of a Young Girl by Anne Frank
Lincoln: A Photobiography by Russell Freedman
The Voice That Challenged a Nation by Russell Freedman
The Wright Brothers by Russell Freedman
And Then What Happened, Paul Revere? by Jean Fritz
From Hand to Mouth by James Cross Giblin
Hitler by James Cross Giblin
It's Perfectly Normal by Robbie Harris
The Endless Steppe by Esther Hautzig
Paddle-to-the-Sea by Holling C. Holling
Rocks in His Head by Carl Otis Hurst
Wilma Unlimited by Kathleen Krull
Harriet and the Promised Land by Jacob Lawrence
Cathedral by David Macaulay
The New Way Things Work by David Macaulay
Snowflake Bentley by Jacqueline Briggs Martin
An American Plague by Jim Murphy
The Boys' War by Jim Murphy
The Great Fire by Jim Murphy
Sequoyah by James Rumford
How Much Is a Million? by David Schwartz
Bard of Avon: The Story of William Shakespeare by Diane Stanley

Multicultural Books
The Winter People by Joseph Bruchac
Sadako and the Thousand Paper Cranes by Eleanor Coerr
The Watsons Go to Birmingham — 1963 by Christopher Paul Curtis
Abuela by Arthur Dorres
Morning Girl by Michael Dorris
Anne Frank: The Diary of a Young Girl by Anne Frank
Honey, I Love by Eloise Greenfield
The People Could Fly by Virginia Hamilton

Zeely by Virginia Hamilton
Breaking Through by Francisco Jiménez
The Circuit by Francisco Jiménez
Julius by Angela Johnson
Hershel and the Hanukkah Goblins by Eric Kimmel
John Henry by Julius Lester
To Be a Slave by Julius Lester
In the Year of the Boar and Jackie Robinson by Bette Bao Lord
In the Hollow of Your Hand by Alice McGill
Molly Bannaky by Alice McGill
Flossie and the Fox by Patricia McKissack
Mirandy and Brother Wind by Patricia McKissack
Baseball Saved Us by Ken Mochizuki
Martin's Big Words by Doreen Rappaport
Grandfather's Journey by Allen Say
Baseball in April and Other Stories by Gary Soto
Chato's Kitchen by Gary Soto
Mufaro's Beautiful Daughters by John Steptoe
Stevie by John Steptoe
Roll of Thunder, Hear My Cry by Mildred Taylor
Tales from Gold Mountain by Paul Yee
Dragonwings by Laurence Yep
The Star Fisher by Laurence Yep

Myths, Legends, and Folklore

Why Mosquitoes Buzz in People's Ears by Verna Aardema
The Naked Bear: Folktales of the Iroquois by John Bierhorst
The Mitten by Jan Brett
Keepers of the Earth by Joseph Bruchac and Michael Caduto
The Jack Tales by Richard Chase
D'Aulaires' Book of Greek Myths by Ingri and Edgar d'Aulaire
Strega Nona by Tomie dePaola
Little Red Riding Hood by Paul Galdone
Snow-White and the Seven Dwarfs by Jacob and Wilhelm Grimm
The People Could Fly by Virginia Hamilton
Paul Bunyan by Steven Kellogg
Uncle Remus by Julius Lester
Aesop's Fables, illustrated by Jerry Pinkney
The Stinky Cheese Man and Other Fairly Stupid Tales by Jon Scieszka
Nursery Tales Around the World by Judy Sierra
Zlateh the Goat and Other Stories by Isaac Bashevis Singer
Arabian Nights by Kate D. Wiggin

Douglas and Lois,

This book was written by a wonderful Simmons teacher. As I was reread it, I realized that part-icularly the book for middle and bolder readers may give you ideas of books you want to read together.

This Oct. she's going to have a similar book on young adult books published.

I hope you enjoy it!

Love, Gma

No. 348 Lupine & Daisies © ANNE KILHAM ROCKPORT, MAINE
DISTRIBUTED BY PEN & INC. OF CONCORD, N.H.

The Rainbow People by Laurence Yep
Seven Blind Mice by Ed Young

Poetry
Bronzeville Boys and Girls by Gwendolyn Brooks
I Met a Man by John Ciardi
Come Hither by Walter de la Mare
Peacock Pie by Walter de la Mare
Joyful Noise: Poems for Two Voices by Paul Fleischman
Dream Keeper and Other Poems by Langston Hughes
The Place My Words Are Looking For by Paul Janeczko
The Complete Nonsense of Edward Lear by Edward Lear
Alligator Pie by Dennis Lee
All Small: Poems by David McCord
Touching the Sky by Naomi Shihab Nye
The Dragons Are Singing Tonight by Jack Prelutsky
The New Kid on the Block by Jack Prelutsky
The Random House Book of Poetry for Children by Jack Prelutsky
Where the Sidewalk Ends by Shel Silverstein
A Child's Garden of Verses by Robert Louis Stevenson
A Visit to William Blake's Inn by Nancy Willard
All the Small Poems by Valerie Worth

Books to Help Locate Other Titles

How to Get Your Child to Love Reading by Esmé Raji Codell
Choosing Books for Children: A Commonsense Guide by Betsy Hearne
Reading for the Love of It by Michele Landsberg
The New York Times Parent's Guide to the Best Books for Children by Eden Ross Lipson
Fantasy Literature for Children and Young Adults by Ruth Nadelman Lynn
Valerie and Walter's Best Books for Children by Valerie Lewis and Walter Mayes
Great Books for Boys by Kathleen Odean
Great Books for Girls by Kathleen Odean
For Reading Out Loud! By Margaret Mary Kimmel and Elizabeth Segel
Children's Books and Their Creators by Anita Silvey
The Essential Guide to Children's Books and Their Creators by Anita Silvey
The Read-Aloud Handbook by Jim Trelease

Bibliography

Adelman, Kenneth L. "Growing Pains." *Washingtonian*. Vol. 33. January 1998.

Anderson, Douglas A. *The Annotated Hobbit. Revised Edition.* Houghton Mifflin, 2002.

Andrews, Terry. *The Story of Harold.* Holt, Rinehart, and Winston, 1974.

Andronik, Catherine M. *Kindred Spirit: A Biography of L. M. Montgomery, Creator of Anne of Green Gables.* Atheneum, 1993.

Angell, Roger. "The Minstrel Steig." *The New Yorker.* February 20 and 27, 1995.

Apseloff, Marilyn Fain. *Elizabeth George Speare.* Twayne, 1991.

Babbitt, Natalie. Manuscript for *Tuck Everlasting.* Thomas J. Dodd Research Center, University of Connecticut, Storrs.

Bader, Barbara. "How the Little House Gave Ground." *Horn Book Magazine.* November 2002.

———. *American Picturebooks from Noah's Ark to the Beast Within.* Macmillan, 1976.

Bales, Jack. *Esther Forbes: A Bio-Bibliography of the Author of Johnny Tremain.* Scarecrow Press, 1998.

Bemelmans, Ludwig. *Mad About Madeline.* Viking, 1993.

Bloom, Susan P., and Cathryn M. Mercier. *Presenting Avi.* Twayne, 1997.

Briggs, Raymond. "The Snowman." *Horn Book Magazine.* January 1980.

Buell, Ellen Lewis. *A Family Treasury of Little Golden Books.* Introduction by Leonard S. Marcus. Golden Books, 1998.

Carle, Eric. *The Art of Eric Carle.* Philomel, 1996.

Carpenter, Humphrey. *Tolkien.* Houghton Mifflin, 1977.

Chaston, Joel D. *Lois Lowry.* Twayne, 1997.

Cleary, Beverly. *A Girl from Yamhill.* Morrow, 1988.

Contemporary Authors. A directory for author information.

Cosgrave, Mary Silva. "Elizabeth George Speare." *Horn Book Magazine.* August 1989.

Cummins, Elizabeth. *Understanding Ursula K. Le Guin.* University of South Carolina Press, 1990.

DiCamillo, Kate. Manuscript for *Because of Winn-Dixie.* Kerlan Collection, University of Minnesota, Minneapolis.

Dorris, Michael. "Rewriting History." *Paper Trail*. HarperCollins, 1994.

Dunleavy, M. P. "The Bedeviled Swamp Angel." *Publishers Weekly*. November 28, 1994.

Eager, Edward. *Dictionary of Literary Biography*. Vol. 22. Gale Research, 1983.

Elleman, Barbara. *Virginia Lee Burton: A Life in Art*. Houghton Mifflin, 2002.

Estes, Eleanor. Manuscript for *The Hundred Dresses*. Kerlan Collection, University of Minnesota, Minneapolis.

Fleischman, Sid. "Humbug Mountain." *Horn Book Magazine*. January 1980.

———. Manuscript for *Humbug Mountain*. Kerlan Collection, University of Minnesota, Minneapolis.

———. *The Abracadabra Kid: A Writer's Life*. Greenwillow Books, 1996.

Forbes, Esther. "Newbery Medal Acceptance Speech." *Horn Book Magazine*. August 1944.

Gág, Wanda. Manuscript and artwork for *Millions of Cats*. Kerlan Collection, University of Minnesota, Minneapolis.

Gardiner, John Reynolds. *Claremont Reading Conference 51st Yearbook*. Claremont Graduate School, 1987.

George, Jean Craighead. "Newbery Medal Acceptance Speech." *Horn Book Magazine*. August 1973.

———. Manuscript for *Julie of the Wolves*. Kerlan Collection, University of Minnesota, Minneapolis.

Hanks, Dorrel Thomas, Jr. *E. L. Konigsburg*. Twayne, 1992.

Harrison, Barbara, and Gregory Maguire. *Origins of Story*. McElderry, 1999.

Hearne, Michael Patrick, Trinkett Clark, and H. Nicholas B. Clark. *Myth, Magic, and Mystery*. Roberts Rinehart, 1996.

Henry, Marguerite. *A Pictorial Life Story of Misty*. Rand McNally, 1976.

———. Manuscript for *Misty of Chincoteague*. Kerlan Collection, University of Minnesota, Minneapolis.

Hepperman, Christine. "A Zest for Life Animates This Artist's Menagerie of Characters." *Riverback Review*. Summer 2002.

Holtz, William. *The Ghost in the Little House: A Life of Rose Wilder Lane*. University of Missouri Press, 1993.

Hopkins, Lee. *More Books by More People*. Macmillan, 1974.

Junior Book of Authors. A bibliographical guide to writers and illustrators of children's books.

King-Smith, Dick. *Chewing the Cud*. Knopf, 2002.

Kraus, Robert. Manuscript for *Leo the Late Bloomer*. Kerlan Collection, University of Minnesota, Minneapolis.

Lamb, Brian. Interview with Bette Bao Lord. *Booknotes.* May 27, 1990.

Lanes, Selma G. *The Art of Maurice Sendak.* Harry Abrams, 1980.

Larkin, David. *The Art of Nancy Ekholm Burkert.* Introduction by Michael Danoff. Harper and Row, 1977.

Le Guin, Ursula K. "Earthsea Revisioned." *Children's Literature New England.* Green Bay Publications, 1993.

L'Engle, Madeleine. *A Circle of Quiet.* Farrar, Straus and Giroux, 1972.

———. Manuscript for *A Wrinkle in Time.* DeGrummond Collection, University of Southern Mississippi, Hattiesburg.

Lionni, Leo. *Between Worlds.* Knopf, 1997.

Lobel, Arnold. "Frog and Toad: A Short History." *Claremont Reading Conference 42nd Yearbook.* Claremont Graduate School, 1978.

Lowry, Lois. Manuscript for *The Giver.* Kerlan Collection, University of Minnesota, Minneapolis.

Lurie, Alison. *Boys and Girls Forever.* Penguin Books, 2003.

Macaulay, David. *The Building of the Book Cathedral.* Houghton Mifflin, 1999.

———. "Newbery Medal Acceptance Speech." *Horn Book Magazine.* July 1991.

MacLachlan, Patricia. "Newbery Medal Acceptance Speech." *Horn Book Magazine.* July 1986.

Manlove, Colin. *The Chronicles of Narnia: The Patterning of a Fantastic World.* Twayne, 1993.

Marciano, John Bemelmans. *Bemelmans: The Life and Art of Madeline's Creator.* Viking, 1999.

Marcus, Leonard S. *A Caldecott Celebration.* Walker, 1998.

———. *Dear Genius: The Letters of Ursula Nordstrom.* HarperCollins, 1998.

———. *Margaret Wise Brown: Awakened by the Moon.* Beacon Press, 1992.

———. *Side by Side.* Walker, 2001.

———. *Storied City: A Children's Book Walking-Tour Guide to New York City.* Dutton, 2003

———. *The Making of Goodnight Moon: A 50th Anniversary Retrospective.* HarperCollins, 1997.

———. *Ways of Telling.* Dutton, 2002.

Marshall, James. Sketch Book no. 24. Thomas J. Dodd Research Center, University of Connecticut, Storrs.

McDonnell, Christine. "Sylvia Cassedy: Valuing the Child's Inner Life." *Horn Book Magazine.* January 1991.

Menand, Louis. "Cat People: What Dr. Seuss Really Taught Us." *The New Yorker.* December 23 and 30, 2002.

Mikkelsen, Nina. *Susan Cooper.* Twayne, 1998.

Milne, Christopher. *The Enchanted Places.* E. P. Dutton, 1975.

Morgan, Judith and Neil. *Dr. Seuss and Mr. Geisel: A Biography.* Da Capo Press, 1996.

Natov, Roni, and Geraldine DeLuca. "An Interview with Philippa Pearce." *The Lion and the Unicorn.* 1985.

Nel, Philip. "Crockett Johnson and Ruth Krauss: A Biography." Unpublished manuscript. Department of English, Kansas State University, Mahattan, Kansas.

———. *J. K. Rowling's Harry Potter Novels.* Continuum, 2001.

Neumeyer, Peter F. *The Annotated Charlotte's Web.* HarperCollins, 1994.

North, Sterling. *Raccoons Are the Brightest People.* E. P. Dutton, 1996.

O'Dell, Scott. *Island of the Blue Dolphins.* Introduction by Zena Sutherland. Houghton Mifflin, 1990.

———. "Newbery Medal Acceptance Speech." *Horn Book Magazine.* August 1961.

Paterson, Katherine. "Newbery Medal Acceptance Speech." *Horn Book Magazine.* August 1978.

———. "Still Summoned by Books." Lecture delivered at UCLA Department of Library and Information Science. 1998.

Penguin Book of Classic Children's Characters. Introduction by Leonard S. Marcus. Dutton, 1997.

Raskin, Ellen. "Newbery Medal Acceptance Speech." *Horn Book Magazine.* August 1979.

Reid, Suzanne Elizabeth. *Presenting Cynthia Voigt.* Twayne, 1995.

Rylant, Cynthia. *But I'll Be Back Again: An Album.* Orchard, 1989.

Sendak, Maurice. "Caldecott Medal Acceptance Speech." *Horn Book Magazine.* August 1964.

Shannon, George. *Arnold Lobel.* Twayne, 1989.

Silvey, Anita. *Children's Books and Their Creators.* Houghton Mifflin, 1995.

———. *The Essential Guide to Children's Books and Their Creators.* Houghton Mifflin, 2002.

———. "An Interview with Cynthia Rylant." *Horn Book Magazine.* November 1987.

Something About the Author. A biographical and bibliographical guide to writers and illustrators of children's books.

Speare, Elizabeth George. "Newbery Medal Acceptance Speech." *Horn Book Magazine.* August 1959.

Spivack, Charlotte. *Ursula K. Le Guin.* Twayne, 1984.

Stavitsky, Gail. *Slobodkina: The Life and Art of Esphyr Slobodkina.* Tufts University Art Gallery, 1992.

Stone, RoseEtta. Interview with Norton Juster. *Absolute Write*. December 18, 2001.

Sutton, Roger. "An Interview with Russell Freedman." *Horn Book Magazine*. November 2002.

Townsend, John Rowe. *A Sense of Story: Essays on Contemporary Writers for Children*. J. B. Lippincott, 1971.

Van Allsburg, Chris. "Caldecott Medal Acceptance Speech." *Horn Book Magazine*. July 1986.

Weiss, Jacqueline Shachter. *Profiles in Children's Literature: Discussions with Authors, Artists, and Editors*. Scarecrow Press, 2001.

Whalen, Sharla Scannell. *The Betsy-Tacy Companion: A Biography of Maud Hart Lovelace*. Portalington Press, 1995.

White, E. B. *Charlotte's Web. 50th Anniversary Retrospective Edition*. Afterword by Peter F. Neumeyer. HarperCollins, 2002.

Williams, Vera B. "Some Thoughts on Writing and Illustrating." Children's Book Council Archives.

Wilson, A. N. *C. S. Lewis: A Biography*. Ballantine Books, 1991.

Young, Ed. "Caldecott Medal Acceptance Speech." *Horn Book Magazine*. July 1990.

———. Manuscript and art for *Seven Blind Mice*. Thomas J. Dodd Research Center, University of Connecticut, Storrs.

Zion, Gene. Manuscript for *Harry the Dirty Dog*. Kerlan Collection, University of Minnesota, Minneapolis.

Personal Interviews and Correspondence

Bicknell, Liz. Interview about *Because of Winn-Dixie*. February 24, 2003.

Bowen, Brenda. Interview about *Out of the Dust*. May 12, 2003.

Brooks, Donna. E-mail correspondence about *Swamp Angel*. March 17, 2003.

Cosgrave, Mary Silva. Interview about *The Witch of Blackbird Pond*. February 20, 2003.

Ehlert, Lois. Interview about *Chicka Chicka Boom Boom*. January 16, 2003.

Fenton, Barbara. Interview about *Stone Fox*. April 30, 2003.

Foster, Frances. Interview about *Holes*. June 18, 2003.

Gauch, Patricia Lee. Interview about *Redwall*. February 6, 2003.

———. Interview about *Seven Blind Mice*. February 24, 2003.

Graham, Margaret Bloy. Interviews about *Harry the Dirty Dog*. March 3, 2003, and April 17, 2003.

Hayes, Regina. Interview about *The True Story of the 3 Little Pigs*. May 12, 2003.

Hirschman, Susan. Interview about *Frog and Toad Are Friends, The New Kid on the Block, Little Bear, Leo the Late Bloomer, A Chair for My Mother,* and *Lilly's Purple Plastic Purse*. February 27, 2003.

Hurd, Thacher. Interview about *Goodnight Moon*. August 30, 2002.

Keller, John. Interview about *The Incredible Journey*. February 11, 2003.

Kriney, Marilyn. Interview about *Behind the Attic Wall*. May 1, 2003.

Lalicki, Barbara. Interview about *Hatchet*. April 21, 2003.

Levine, Arthur. Interview about *Officer Buckle and Gloria* and *Harry Potter and the Sorcerer's Stone*. February 20, 2003.

Marcus, Leonard S. Interview. February 5, 2003.

McCarthy, Donna. Interview about *Grandfather's Journey*. March 6, 2003.

Murphy, Jim. Interview about *The Great Fire*. July 22, 2002.

Natti, Lee Kingman. Interview about *Johnny Tremain*. January 14, 2000.

Schulman, Janet. Interview about *The People Could Fly*. February 4, 2003.

Stevenson, Dinah. Interview about *Catherine, Called Birdy*. January 30, 2003.

Reading Journal

Alexander and the Terrible, Horrible, No Good, Very Bad Day

Anne Frank: The Diary of a Young Girl

Anne of Green Gables

Babe: The Gallant Pig

Because of Winn-Dixie

Behind the Attic Wall

Betsy-Tacy

The BFG

Bridge to Terabithia

Caps for Sale

The Carrot Seed

The Cat in the Hat

Catherine, Called Birdy

A Chair for My Mother

Charlotte's Web

Chicka Chicka Boom Boom

The Cricket in Times Square

Curious George

The Dark Is Rising

Doctor De Soto

Freight Train

Frog and Toad Are Friends

From the Mixed-up Files of Mrs. Basil E. Frankweiler

The Giver

Goodnight Moon

Grandfather's Journey

The Great Fire

Half Magic

Harriet the Spy

Harry Potter and the Sorcerer's Stone

Harry the Dirty Dog

Hatchet

Henry and Mudge

The Hobbit

Holes

Homecoming

Humbug Mountain

The Hundred Dresses

In the Year of the Boar and Jackie Robinson

The Incredible Journey

Island of the Blue Dolphins

John Henry

Johnny Tremain

Julie of the Wolves

Leo the Late Bloomer

Lilly's Purple Plastic Purse

Lincoln: A Photobiography

The Lion, the Witch, and the Wardrobe

Little Bear

Little House in the Big Woods

Madeline

Make Way for Ducklings

Mary Poppins

Mike Mulligan and His Steam Shovel

Millions of Cats

Miss Nelson Is Missing!

Misty of Chincoteague

Morning Girl

Mr. Gumpy's Outing

Mrs. Frisby and the Rats of NIMH

My Father's Dragon

The New Kid on the Block

The New Way Things Work

Officer Buckle and Gloria

Out of the Dust

The People Could Fly

The Phantom Tollbooth

Pippi Longstocking

The Polar Express

Rabbit Hill

Ramona the Pest

Rascal

Redwall

Roll of Thunder, Hear My Cry

Sadako and the Thousand Paper Cranes

Sarah, Plain and Tall

The Secret Garden

Seven Blind Mice

Snowflake Bentley

The Snowman

Snow-White and the Seven Dwarfs

The Snowy Day

Stone Fox

The Story of Ferdinand

Swamp Angel

Swimmy

The Tale of Peter Rabbit

Tom's Midnight Garden

The True Confessions of Charlotte Doyle

The True Story of the 3 Little Pigs

Tuck Everlasting

Tuesday

The Very Hungry Caterpillar

The Westing Game

Where the Wild Things Are

The Wind in the Willows

Winnie-the-Pooh

The Witch of Blackbird Pond

A Wizard of Earthsea

A Wrinkle in Time

Personal Favorites

BOOK/DATE READ/COMMENTS

BOOK/DATE READ/COMMENTS

BOOK/DATE READ/COMMENTS

Index